DISEASES AND DISORDERS

HPV
PREVENTION AND TREATMENT

By Michelle Harris

Portions of this book originally appeared in *Human Papillomavirus (HPV)* by Don Nardo.

LUCENT
PRESS

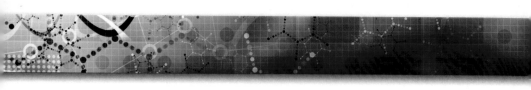

Published in 2019 by
Lucent Press, an Imprint of Greenhaven Publishing, LLC
353 3rd Avenue
Suite 255
New York, NY 10010

Designer: Deanna Paternostro
Editor: Jennifer Lombardo

Library of Congress Cataloging-in-Publication Data

Names: Harris, Michelle, 1986- author.
Title: HPV : prevention and treatment / Michelle Harris.
Description: New York : Lucent Press, [2019] | Series: Diseases and disorders
    | Includes bibliographical references and index.
Identifiers: LCCN 2017061425 (print) | LCCN 2017059774 (ebook) | ISBN
    9781534563711 (eBook) | ISBN 9781534563704 (library bound book) | ISBN
    9781534563728 (paperback book)
Subjects: LCSH: Papillomaviruses–Prevention. | Papillomaviruses–Treatment.
Classification: LCC QR406 (print) | LCC QR406 .H37 2019 (ebook) | DDC
    614.5/81–dc23
LC record available at https://lccn.loc.gov/2017061425

Printed in the United States of America

CPSIA compliance information: Batch #BS18KL: For further information contact Greenhaven Publishing LLC, New York, New York at 1-844-317-7404.

Please visit our website, www.greenhavenpublishing.com. For a free color catalog of all our high-quality books, call toll free 1-844-317-7404 or fax 1-844-317-7405.

CONTENTS

Illness is an unfortunate part of life, and it is one that is often misunderstood. Thanks to advances in science and technology, people have been aware for many years that diseases such as the flu, pneumonia, and chicken pox are caused by viruses and bacteria. These diseases all cause physical symptoms that people can see and understand, and many people have dealt with these diseases themselves. However, sometimes diseases that were previously unknown in most of the world turn into epidemics and spread across the globe. Without an awareness of the method by which these diseases are spread—through the air, through human waste or fluids, through sexual contact, or by some other method—people cannot take the proper precautions to prevent further contamination. Panic often accompanies epidemics as a result of this lack of knowledge.

Knowledge is power in the case of mental disorders, as well. Mental disorders are just as common as physical disorders, but due to a lack of awareness among the general public, they are often stigmatized. Scientists have studied them for years and have found that they are generally caused by hormonal imbalances in the brain, but they have not yet determined with certainty what causes those imbalances or how to fix them. Because even mild mental illness is stigmatized in Western society, many people prefer not to talk about it.

Chronic pain disorders are also not well understood—even by researchers—and do not yet have foolproof treatments. People who have a mental disorder or a disease or disorder that causes them to feel chronic pain can be the target of uninformed opinions. People who do not have these disorders sometimes struggle to understand how difficult it can be to deal with the symptoms. These disorders are often termed "invisible illnesses" because no one can see the symptoms; this leads many people to doubt that they exist or are serious problems. Additionally, people who have an undiagnosed disorder may understand that they are experiencing the world in a different way than their peers, but they have no one to turn to for answers.

Misinformation about all kinds of ailments is often spread through personal anecdotes, social media, and even news sources. This series aims to present accurate information about both physical and mental conditions so young adults will have a better understanding of them. Each volume discusses the symptoms of a particular disease or disorder, ways it is currently being treated, and the research that is being done to understand it further. Advice for people who may be suffering from a disorder is included, as well as information for their loved ones about how best to support them.

With fully cited quotes, a list of recommended books and websites for further research, and informational charts, this series provides young adults with a factual introduction to common illnesses. By learning more about these ailments, they will be better able to prevent the spread of contagious diseases, show compassion to people who are dealing with invisible illnesses, and take charge of their own health.

WHAT IS HPV?

Many people are surprised when they discover that the human papillomavirus (HPV) is actually the most common sexually transmitted disease (STD) in the world. It may not have the name recognition that syphilis, herpes, or human immunodeficiency virus (HIV) have, but most sexually active people do come into contact with it at some point in their lives.

HPV is not, in fact, a single virus; rather, it is a group of more than 100 related viruses that infect the skin. It passes from one person to another through direct skin-to-skin contact, typically via sexual activity. HPV often disappears on its own after about a few months to a year, thanks to the body's immune system, but while a person carries it, they can pass it on to one or more sexual partners, some of whom will become infected.

About 79 million people in the United States are presently infected with HPV, with about 14 million people becoming newly infected every year. Some of these people have or will eventually develop small, harmless warts on their feet, legs, hands, or faces. Others will develop diseases such as genital warts, cervical cancer, or other kinds of cancer.

Considering how widespread HPV is, one would assume that, like gonorrhea, HIV, and herpes, it would be well known among the general population. However, this is not the case; many people have never heard about it. Despite its wide reach, HPV remains one of the least-known STDs people can catch. Unfortunately, this public ignorance can have some serious—sometimes even fatal—consequences.

The Outcast Illness

HPV is not a new disease; in fact, evidence shows that it, and the serious conditions it can cause, have existed throughout human history. Even the ancient Greeks recognized the existence of genital warts. The second-century AD Greek physician Soranus

The ancient Greeks knew about genital warts, but it was not until the 1990s that doctors truly began to understand HPV.

actually wrote an essay titled "On Warty Growths of the Female Genitals." Soranus and his colleagues also recognized that such warts could pass from one person to another during sexual relations; however, they did not understand why, since the germ theory of disease would not be introduced until about 16 centuries later. Even after the discovery in the 1800s that germs (bacteria and viruses) cause disease, doctors did not quite understand HPV or its role in other diseases. Only in the early 1990s was the link between HPV and cervical cancer established beyond the shadow of a doubt. Therefore, while the disease itself is not new, firmly reliable information about it and its consequences has not been available until relatively recently.

Another reason for HPV's lack of name recognition is that it is a fairly low-key infection. There are often few or no symptoms, so patients are not likely to be aware they are infected until later, when warts or cancer develop. The best way to avoid these consequences is to understand how HPV infection occurs, its symptoms, and the key preventive actions sexually active people can take to keep themselves healthy.

A Special Note Regarding Biological Sex and Gender Identity

Before talking about sexually transmitted diseases, it is important to clarify what is meant by a person's sex. Sex is a label, male or female, that is assigned to a person at birth based on the genitals they are born with and their genetic makeup. Gender identity is a person's innermost concept of who they are, whether that is a man, a woman, a blend of both, or neither. For the purposes of this book, the term "female" will refer to all individuals who have a cervix, uterus, and vagina, including transgender

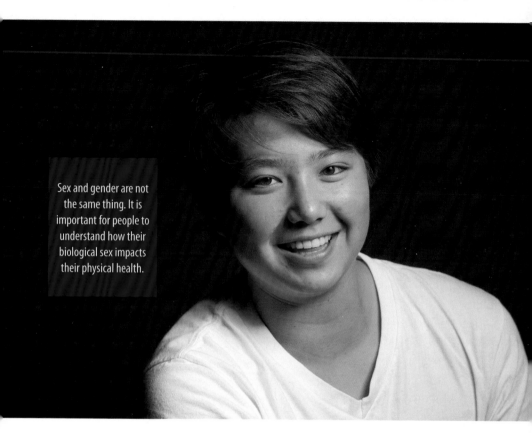

Sex and gender are not the same thing. It is important for people to understand how their biological sex impacts their physical health.

men. The term "male" will refer to all individuals who have a penis and testicles, including transgender women. Since HPV can impact females and males differently, it is important to make this distinction to help ensure everyone understands their individual risk.

CHAPTER ONE

THE TRUTH ABOUT HPV

The human papillomavirus, or HPV, is one of the least understood viruses that affect people. Thanks to its complex and relatively low-key nature, not much was written about HPV prior to the 1980s, when the link between the virus and certain cancers became clearer. In contrast, other viruses that likewise can threaten the general population, such as HIV, herpes, or gonorrhea, have been well documented and researched for decades (and in some cases, centuries), leading to many films, literary references, and television episodes to raise awareness in the general public.

With very little accurate information circulating, it is no wonder that a number of myths have arisen about the virus, particularly about which people are most likely to contract HPV and how the infection spreads.

Common Myths About HPV

With widespread ignorance comes great misunderstanding. HPV runs so far under most people's radar that it has developed many myths in society. One of the most common myths is sometimes called the "I'm the only one" assumption. Most often, a person who discovers that they have contracted HPV has never heard of it prior to that

Can Condoms Prevent an HPV Infection?

The answer to this question is complicated. While condoms can be very (though not 100 percent) effective against STDs that are transmitted through bodily fluids, particularly gonorrhea and HIV, they are not as effective against HPV. This is because a condom, when properly used, captures all, or at least most, of the fluids involved. However, HPV spreads through skin-to-skin contact. As the American Sexual Health Association explained:

> Condoms do not cover the entire genital area. They leave the vulva, anus, perineal area (between the anus and vagina in [females] and between the anus and scrotum in [males]), base of the penis, and scrotum uncovered, and contact between these areas can transmit HPV … That is not to say condoms are useless. In fact, studies have shown condom use can lower the risk of acquiring HPV infection and reduce the risk of HPV-related diseases, as well as help prevent other STDs and unintended pregnancy.[1]

Condoms help prevent pregnancy and the spread of many STDs, but they are less effective at preventing the spread of HPV.

1. "HPV: Myths and Facts," American Sexual Health Association.www.ashasexualhealth.org/stdsstis/hpv/hpv-myths-facts/.

moment. The person therefore assumes that if the virus were common, they would have heard people talk about it before. At one time or another, for instance, nearly everybody has heard others mention or talk about HIV (or AIDS, which HIV can lead to) or gonorrhea. Therefore, the person reasons, an HPV infection must be very rare and they have had the misfortune to catch a disease that medical science does not understand well and may not be able to treat. Not surprisingly, this assumption can cause a great deal of anxiety. "I was terrified after my doctor told me I had it,"[1] said Karen, who contracted HPV in 2006. She explained,

> *He didn't mention how common it was ... only that I must have gotten it from sex. I never heard anybody mention it before, so I figured very few people got it, which could mean there's either no really effective treatment for it or else I might end up as some kind of guinea pig while the doctors experimented with new treatments and stuff. Until I went out and read up on HPV for myself, I was ... [such] a nervous wreck that I had trouble sleeping.[2]*

In reality, however, the reason Karen and others like her have not heard people talk about HPV before is simply that people are reluctant to talk about it. "Those struggling with this troubling condition or strange new diagnosis rarely discuss it with others," the American Sexual Health Association (ASHA) pointed out,

> *since it would seem unlikely that they would understand. And others—your second-best friend, your cousin, your coworker, your neighbor across the street—likewise feel constrained to keep silent about their HPV, thinking that*

you wouldn't understand. The net result is that very few people ever have the chance to place genital HPV in an accurate context, as the very common virus it really is.[3]

Indeed, HPV is far from rare. The Centers for Disease Control and Prevention (CDC) reported that as of 2017, nearly 80 million people, or one in four, are infected with HPV in the United States. In fact, most sexually active

Because of persistent myths about HPV, many people think it is a rare disease and are very scared when they receive a diagnosis.

people will get at least one type of HPV at some point in their lives. More than 14 million Americans are newly infected with HPV each year, so any person who is diagnosed with an HPV infection need not fear that they are alone. Granted, the CDC and other authorities on STDs caution that a majority of those who do become infected with HPV remain so only briefly—a few months to a year or two. However, a significant number remain infected longer. Of these, some develop unpleasant or dangerous physical ailments.

How HPV Infections Occur

Another common myth about HPV relates to how it can spread from one person to another. Because the virus is so often classified as an STD, a common misconception is that someone has to engage in sexual activity to contract the disease. However, the reality is often quite different. Although some versions of the HPV virus specifically target the genital area, the majority of HPV viruses do not. For example, some cause ordinary warts, including plantar warts on the feet, and do not generally spread through sexual contact. In general, infection by HPV occurs through the skin, most often from one person's skin to another person's skin. More important, the point of contact in which the infection occurs does not have to be in the genital area (although it quite often is). Any exposed patch of skin is vulnerable to one version or another of the virus.

To understand how the HPV virus actually invades the skin, it is important to have some basic knowledge about viruses and how they operate. Viruses are the smallest of the many different kinds of germs, including bacteria, protozoa, and others. In fact, an average virus is thousands of times smaller than an average bacterium, which is itself microscopic. This means viruses are visible only under very

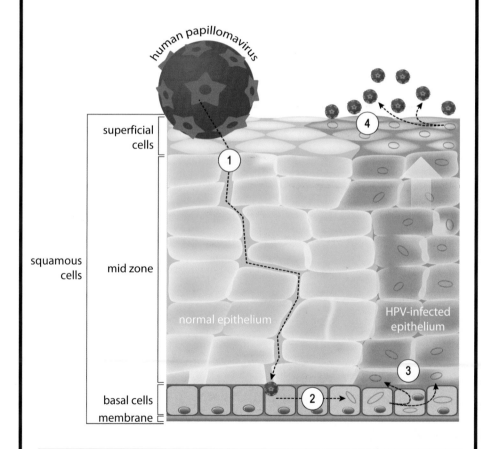

The Life Cycle of HPV

human papillomavirus

superficial cells

squamous cells

mid zone

normal epithelium

HPV-infected epithelium

basal cells

membrane

1. The virus invades epithelial layers
2. Infected basal cell
3. HPV in epithelial cells
4. Viral replication

This diagram shows what happens when the HPV virus comes in contact with a person's skin and finds its way into a small opening in the top layer of cells, which is called the superficial layer.

powerful microscopes. These tiny germs are essentially thin, twisted strands with a surprisingly simple makeup. Each consists of a bit of protein and a touch of a chemical called nucleic acid.

Unlike most other types of germs, viruses cannot reproduce on their own. They can reproduce only inside the cells of living organisms (plants or animals), just like parasites. Once a virus has invaded a host cell, it can, through reproduction, spread and take up residence in nearby cells. In this way, a viral disease can steadily spread through a host plant or animal.

In the case of HPV, the virus is particularly tough. It can live for an undetermined length of time—at least several hours and perhaps several days—on the skin's surface (though it cannot reproduce outside of a cell). Millions of viruses can attach themselves to a single outer skin cell, called a squamous cell.

The Invasion Begins

Once a virus has entered a host body, it has to start reproducing itself in order to establish an infection. In order to do this, the virus needs to reach the cells in the lower layer of the skin, which are called basal cells. These cells are constantly dividing and creating fresh skin cells, making them prime targets for a hostile takeover by a sinister virus. So how does the virus get there? The HPV viral strands reach these basal cells by entering tiny tears or scratches in the outer layers of the skin, which most people get regularly in their day-to-day lives by bumping into or rubbing up against ordinary objects. Such injuries are often too small to see or feel, and they

HPV in the Throat

Rarely, an infection of two particular strains, or types, of HPV—HPV 6 or 11—can cause tumors to grow in the air passages from the nose and the mouth to the lungs—a condition called recurrent respiratory papillomatosis (RRP). The tumors can vary in size and grow quickly, and they often grow back after removal. When the tumors grow on the larynx, or voice box, it is called laryngeal papillomatosis. RRP affects fewer than 2,000 children per year, who contract it as they are being born, according to the CDC. Researchers are unsure exactly how adults get it, but they believe it is due to sexual contact, the way other forms of the virus are passed on.

Laryngeal papillomatosis may cause hoarseness and difficulty breathing and swallowing in children. Affected adults also experience frequent coughing or hoarseness. To treat the condition, doctors sometimes remove the growths using traditional surgery. Increasingly, however, laser surgery—using a carbon dioxide laser—is also being employed. Unfortunately, even after surgery, the growths can grow back, requiring the patient to undergo additional surgeries. In extreme cases, doctors perform a tracheotomy (make an incision in the throat) and insert a small tube to help the patient breathe.

Some children who are born to mothers with HPV develop growths on their throat, but this is relatively rare.

heal within minutes or hours. However, before they heal, they offer an opening to invading HPV germs. The virus can even more easily invade the body by settling in the moist mucous membranes inside the mouth, throat, nose, vagina, penis, and rectum.

After the virus has made its way into the cells of a host body, it can, under the right circumstances, spread to other parts of that body. For instance, if a person develops a wart on one finger, the HPV viruses in the wart can easily spread to adjacent fingers when the fingers touch. Similarly, touching a plantar wart on the foot can spread the virus to the fingers or other parts of the body. Some HPV viruses can establish themselves in the genital area, too. One person (A) can pass these germs on to their partner (B) simply by touching, either by A's genital area contacting B's genital area directly, or by a finger first touching A's genital area and then touching B's. This means a genital HPV infection can occur even when full or partial sexual intercourse does not occur.

In fact, HPV viruses are so hardy and can spread so readily that doctors must take special precautions when operating on HPV-infected patients. One example, described here by doctor and research scientist Gregory S. Henderson, is removal of genital warts with a laser:

> *During this procedure, surgeons and operating room staff must wear a special ultra-filter mask because even in the vapor that is generated from the lasered warts, infective viruses can survive and enter the nasal passages and upper respiratory tracts. They can take up residence in the nose, mouth, throat, and*

respiratory tract, causing warty lesions [sores] in these areas too.[4]

The Difference Between Dormant and Active Infections

Another common myth about HPV involves its incubation period, or how long a person is infected with a virus before symptoms begin. This myth has likely caused many a heated argument within monogamous couples and resulted in many hurt feelings. According to the myth, if someone in a monogamous relationship (one confined to two people) is diagnosed with an HPV-related disease, it means one of the partners has cheated. This misconception is based partly on the mistaken idea that the virus is contracted only through intimate sexual contact. The fact is that it could also have been passed along unknowingly through casual skin-to-skin contact in a school, office, or other public setting.

The cheating myth is also based on the notion that the HPV virus always leads to the development of warts, cancer, or some other serious condition very soon after entering the body. This can happen, but more often, the virus, having entered the body, lays low or remains dormant. It can remain more or less inactive and undetected for several months or even a few years. Therefore, even if HPV did enter the body through sexual contact, the infection could have occurred long before the beginning of the monogamous relationship in question. This is why, even if someone is in a long-term monogamous relationship, both partners should continue to receive regular STD screenings. Furthermore, everyone should get tested for STDs before becoming sexually active with every new partner. Although an HPV infection may not be detected right away, regular STD testing will help ensure that if someone has contracted an infection of any kind, they receive timely treatment and can avoid passing something along to their partner. It is important to note that there is not yet an effective HPV test for males, so even if a person's male partner has been tested for STDs with negative results, that does not mean an HPV infection is not present.

It is not clear why HPV quickly becomes active in some people and remains long dormant in others. It could be due to differences in the various strains of the virus. Other factors determining the speed and severity of an HPV attack could be the genetic background, everyday behaviors, and emotional well-being of the infected person. For some people, in part because of their genetic makeup, their parents and grandparents tended to have low risks of catching various diseases. The infected person may have inherited these "good" genes. If so, they may have a low risk of developing cancer despite the presence of HPV in their body. Also, behaviors such as smoking and poor diet are known to increase the likelihood of developing cancer and other diseases, as is persistent mental stress. Thus, it may be that people who have favorable genetic backgrounds, eat nutritious foods, do not smoke, and experience little stress are less likely to experience serious complications of the HPV virus.

"High Risk" versus "Low Risk" Strains

As mentioned earlier, there are more than 100 different strains of HPV, and about 40 of them can infect the genitals, mouth, and throat. While some strains of the virus are not harmful and typically go away on their own, others can have serious health consequences. For example, about 360,000 people get genital warts each year. Several million others develop other kinds of warts, such as plantar warts on the soles of

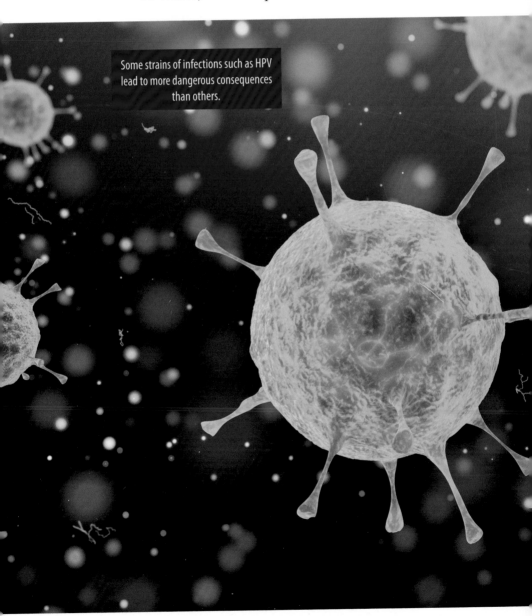

Some strains of infections such as HPV lead to more dangerous consequences than others.

the feet, and roughly 10,000 to 12,000 women develop cervical cancer caused by HPV. Of these, more than 4,000 die. In addition, a few thousand people with HPV go on to develop other cancers, including anal cancer, cancer of the penis, cancer of the mouth, head and neck cancers, and others.

Each of these consequences of HPV is caused by a different strain of the virus. Each strain is designated by a number. For instance, HPV version or strain 1 is associated with plantar warts. HPV 2, 6, 11, and 16 are known to cause genital warts, while oral cancers are associated with HPV 16, 18, 36, and 57. A number of HPV strains are sometimes called "high risk" because they can lead to cervical, penile, anal, and other cancers. These strains include HPV 16, 18, 31, 33, 35, 45, 51, 52, 59, and 68, among others. In contrast, HPV 42, 43, 44, and a few others are considered "low risk" because they generally do not result in these more dangerous consequences.

The Societal Cost of HPV

HPV is highly contagious, and it spreads easily and quickly, which is why it impacts so many people. Although many who are infected with the virus may be unaware and relatively unaffected, it can have very serious consequences for thousands of others.

The monetary costs of HPV for society are also great. According to a report published in the journal *Vaccine*, an estimated $6.6 billion was spent in the United States for routine cervical cancer screenings and follow-up in 2010 alone. An additional $1.5 billion was spent on treatment for HPV-related diseases, including cancer, genital warts, and respiratory disease. There are also the large hidden and uncalculated costs of millions of lost work hours for those who go to doctors or hospitals for testing or treatment. Whether directly or indirectly, HPV affects nearly everyone in society, more often than not in unwanted ways.

CHAPTER TWO
DETECTING HPV INFECTIONS

With most illnesses, individuals are their own first line of defense. Knowing their body well and being able to notice and recognize symptoms are extremely important. For instance, when someone wakes up feverish and achy, with a runny nose and sore throat, they know they likely have the flu. Describing these symptoms to their doctor would then help them provide a diagnosis and a prescription for rest, fluids, and a marathon of the patient's favorite television show. With HPV, however, the virus often presents no obvious symptoms. Patients may find small warts or lesions (sores) on or around their vagina, anus, penis, hands, foot, mouth, or other areas soon after infection occurs, but this is not generally the case.

In the vast majority of cases of HPV in humans, one of two things happens. In the first and most common scenario, the virus remains dormant and hidden and eventually is defeated by the immune system. In the less common but more dangerous scenario, over time, the virus causes cells in the infected area to become abnormal in various ways. These abnormal cells are sometimes labeled "precancerous" because they can—but do not always—later develop into some form of cancer. Such abnormalities are not generally accompanied by noticeable symptoms. In most cases, the

A Revolutionary Test

The inventor of the Pap smear, George N. Papanicolaou, was born on the Greek island of Euboea in 1883. He earned a medical degree in Athens in 1904 and moved with his wife to the United States in 1913. He earned widespread recognition for his studies of the human reproductive tract at New York Hospital and Cornell Medical College. His most famous achievement was his screening test for cervical cancer. He first conceived it in the 1920s, but there was little interest in the medical community at the time. The situation changed, however, after he discussed the concept in his groundbreaking 1943 book, *Diagnosis of Uterine Cancer by the Vaginal Smear*. The idea of the Pap smear, named for him, rapidly caught on with other American doctors. By the 1950s, the use of Pap smears was widespread in the United States and several other countries. Papanicolaou died in 1962. In 1978, the U.S. government honored his memory by publishing a stamp bearing his portrait.

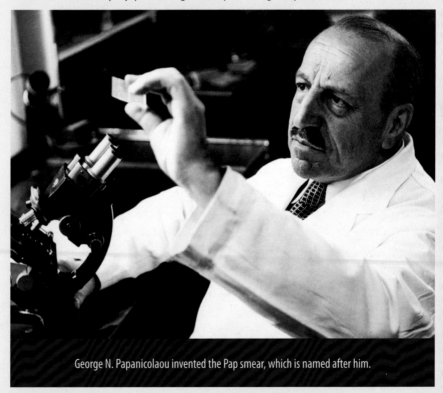

George N. Papanicolaou invented the Pap smear, which is named after him.

infected area does not swell, change color, or itch, so the person may not realize they have cancer until it is too late.

Thankfully, doctors and medical researchers have developed highly effective screening tests to help people avoid this unfortunate outcome. A screening test is not a specific diagnostic test, but rather a first step in the diagnostic process. According to Gregory S. Henderson,

> *The purpose of a screening test is to survey a very large at-risk population and narrow down the individuals who may be suffering from the disease or condition being investigated. Once the screening test has highlighted people with a possible problem, diagnostic tests can determine whether an actual problem is there, and if so, what it is ... In other words, the goal of a screening test is to avoid subjecting a very large group of people to diagnostic tests, which can often be more invasive, uncomfortable, and expensive.*[5]

The Pap Smear Screening

The most common screening test for HPV and HPV-related cancers in females is called the Pap smear, named after the Greek doctor who developed the test, George Papanicolaou. Introduced in 1949, the Pap smear is extremely effective and reliable. In fact, according to the National Institutes of Health (NIH), the incidence and mortality rates of cervical cancer dropped by more than 60 percent between 1955 and 1992, thanks largely to the widespread use of the Pap smear. Once the most common cancer affecting females in the United States, cervical cancer now ranks 14th in frequency.

The general purpose of a Pap smear is to detect HPV-related abnormalities in the cells in a person's skin. In particular, a Pap smear can flag the presence of a precancerous condition. It can also show simply that an active HPV infection is present. A Pap smear is almost always administered in the area of the cervix, located inside the vagina. However, the same basic procedure can be and is occasionally done in the anal area of both females and males who are at high risk for developing abnormal cells in that area.

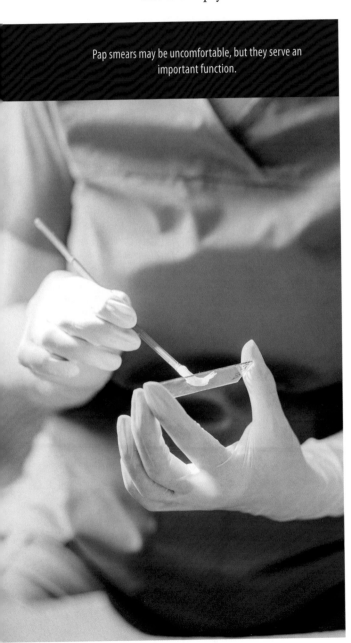

Pap smears may be uncomfortable, but they serve an important function.

The CDC recommends every female between the ages of 21 and 65 undergo a Pap smear every three years, regardless of whether they are sexually active. A person's doctor may advise more frequent testing if abnormal cells are detected. After age 65, if previous Pap tests have been negative and the physician approves, a patient may elect to discontinue the procedure. According to the CDC, between 2010 and 2013, approximately 80 percent of females between the ages of 21 and 65 received a Pap smear.

What happens during a Pap test? While the patient lies on their back on the examination table, the doctor or nurse will carefully insert a speculum (a metal or plastic device that spreads and holds open the vaginal walls), which allows them to see and reach the cervix, the narrow opening of the lower uterus. Then, they gently scrape the cervix's surface using a small, spatula-like instrument and brush the loosened cells onto a glass slide using a small brush. This process generally only takes a few minutes and should not be painful. The patient may experience some discomfort or pressure when the speculum is opened inside the vagina and may also feel a light scratching when the cells are taken from the cervix.

How Pap Smears Are Interpreted

Once a patient's Pap test is completed, the slide holding their extracted cervical cells is taken to a lab for analysis. In the lab, a cytotechnologist—a technician who studies cells—stains the slide with liquids called Papanicolaou stains, which make it easier to see the various parts of each cell. The technician then places the slide under a microscope to examine the cells and check for any abnormalities.

Most often—at least 90 percent of the time— the cytotechnologist sees no abnormalities in the sample cells. These samples are therefore labeled "negative," meaning normal. However, when abnormal-looking cells are found on the slide, the technician uses an ink pen to make a tiny dot next to each suspect cell. In most labs, as a precaution, a second cytotechnologist reviews 10 percent of the Pap smears labeled "negative" by the first one. If any mistakes were made in the first examination, the review generally catches them.

The slide with the questionable cells next goes to a pathologist—a doctor who is an expert at

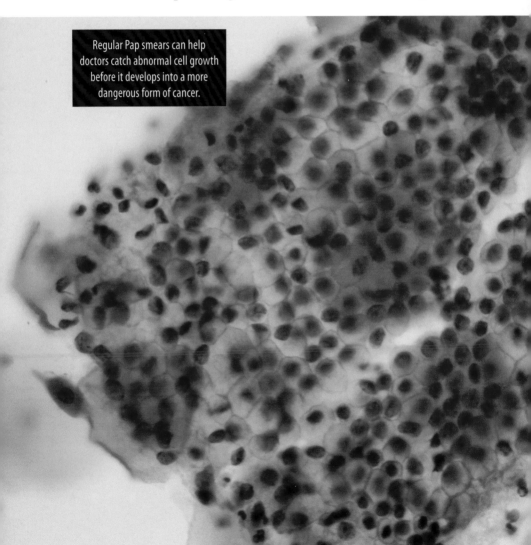

Regular Pap smears can help doctors catch abnormal cell growth before it develops into a more dangerous form of cancer.

recognizing changes and abnormalities in cells, tissues, and organs. The pathologist can confirm whether the cells the cytotechnologist pinpointed are indeed abnormal, and if they are, can determine the severity using the Bethesda Classification System. This system, first created in 1988, provides clear and standard terminology for medical professionals to use to describe the kind of abnormality detected in cells, as well as the severity, which helps doctors determine the best course of care for their patient. The Bethesda Classification System has been revised several times since its original publication, most recently in 2014.

Understanding the Results

Abnormal or unclear Pap test results are fairly common and do not necessarily signal that the patient has cancer. An abnormal test result means that abnormal changes were detected on the cervix, which can range from minor to serious. Minor changes are classified as low-grade, meaning an HPV infection is present, but the infection is in an early stage and not yet precancerous. The most common approach in such cases is "watch and wait," meaning the doctor will order further Pap smears over the next several months, which will be carefully evaluated. Hopefully, during that time, the patient's immune system will get rid of the HPV on its own. Rarely, a doctor may recommend surgical removal of the lesion as a precaution. In such cases, further Pap smears are taken to make sure no abnormal cells have returned.

A more worrisome level in the Pap smear classification scale is high-grade, which indicates moderate or severe dysplasia, a precancerous condition. In cases in which a Pap test indicates moderate or severe dysplasia, the lesion is always surgically removed.

Sometimes Pap smears produce results that do not fall into the negative, low-grade, or high-grade categories. These cells are classified as unclear or "atypical squamous cells of undetermined significance (ASCUS)."[6] According to Planned Parenthood, "an unclear test result means that your cervical cells look like they could be abnormal. But it isn't clear if it's related to HPV or something else."[7] An ASCUS lesion or abnormality might be caused by HPV, but it can have several other causes, including hormonal changes in the body, side effects of certain medications, and even a deficiency of the B vitamin folic acid in the diet. To determine the real cause of ASCUS, doctors generally move on to the next steps in the diagnostic process.

What Comes Next?

If a patient's results show atypical or high-grade cell changes, their doctor will request further testing to definitively diagnose the stage of the HPV infection, which will help determine the course of treatment. The next standard tests used to diagnose HPV are called colposcopy and biopsy.

A colposcopy involves an instrument called a colposcope, which is a special portable microscope equipped with a very bright light. For this test, the doctor first coats the cervix with a solution of vinegar and iodine to make any lesions present more visible. Then the colposcope is carefully inserted, allowing the doctor to closely examine the tissues of the cervix.

If the colposcopy reveals any lesions, even very small ones, the doctor next performs a biopsy. A biopsy is the removal of a small piece of tissue from an area of the body under examination, in this case the cervix. The removed tissue is placed on a slide and given to a pathologist to examine.

The benefit of taking such a sample is that it includes cells from the base of the cervical tissue as well as its surface, giving a much fuller picture of the infected area. Thus, with a tissue sample from a biopsy, a pathologist can confirm

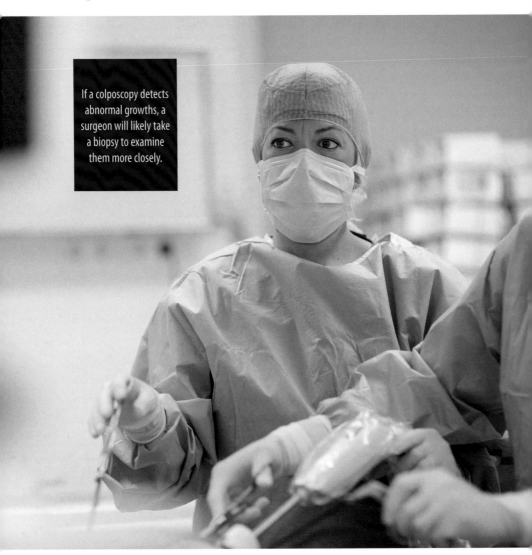

If a colposcopy detects abnormal growths, a surgeon will likely take a biopsy to examine them more closely.

the stage of HPV infection with a high degree of accuracy. At this point, in most cases, the diagnosis is complete.

Getting Tested

People have a few options for where they can go for STD testing, depending on their income and whether they have health insurance. They can go to their primary care doctor or gynecologist's office to get tested, or they can go to a community clinic, the local health department, or a local Planned Parenthood health center.

Many people worry about the cost of getting tested, especially if they do not have health insurance. Some teens choose not to get tested because even though they are covered under their parents' health insurance, they do not want their parents to see the bill and realize that their child is sexually active. However, these fears should not keep someone from getting tested. Most health insurance plans cover STD testing, so the patient may be able to get tested for free or at a reduced price. Testing is also free or available at a low cost with Medicaid coverage and other government programs. Additionally, most local health clinics offer free or low-cost STD tests, depending on a person's income. Talking to a doctor or worker at a local clinic can help someone figure out the best option for them.

Getting tested regularly for STDs is an important part of engaging in responsible sexual activity.

HPV Genetic Tests

In recent years, the Food and Drug Administration (FDA) has approved a number of tests that are able to detect the genetic makeup of specific HPV types. For instance, the Hybrid Capture 2 High-Risk HPV DNA test and the Cervista HPV High-Risk DNA test can detect the presence of about 14 types of HPV that are known to cause cancer. These tests can be performed at the same time as a Pap smear—a process called co-testing—to clarify abnormal Pap results or as a follow-up to treatment for cervical precancers.

Samples for the HPV tests are collected in the same manner as those for Pap smears: A doctor scrapes some cells from the cervix onto a slide. However, instead of examining the cells under a microscope, the lab technicians analyze them to determine their genetic components. If any of the cells in the sample are infected with HPV, the test being performed will determine the specific type of HPV. These tests have at least one advantage over the traditional Pap smear: They can identify infected cells before they have developed enough dysplasia to be visible to technicians examining a Pap smear.

According to the CDC, although HPV genetic tests may eventually become the primary cervical cancer screening, "no such recommendation has been made by any medical organization."[8] It is important to note that positive Pap and HPV tests can detect the early signs of cervical cancer, which typically does not cause noticeable symptoms in patients until it is advanced. If someone receives a positive result, they need to discuss follow-up treatment and testing with their doctor to ensure cervical cancer does not develop.

HPV in Males

Most of the discussion about HPV diagnosis is centered around females, but what about males? According to the CDC, most males who get HPV never develop symptoms, and the infection clears up on its own. However, it can cause genital warts or certain kinds of cancer, and it can still be passed on to that person's sexual partner. Currently, there is no screening test for HPV in males, so physicians typically screen patients with a visual inspection of the genital region. Some health care providers do offer anal Pap tests to males who are at increased risk for anal cancer.

Since there is no FDA-approved screening test for HPV in males, it is important to utilize safe sex practices, including the use of condoms, and to be aware of any changes on or around the genital area. Any new or unusual growths, lumps, sores, or warts on the penis, scrotum, anus, mouth, or throat should be examined by a physician.

A recent study emphasizes the need for further research to develop better methods of screening for HPV in males. The 2017 study, published in the journal *Annals of Internal Medicine*, reported that an estimated 11 million American males, or about one in nine, are infected with cancer-causing oral HPV, compared with 3.2 million females.

"The rates of oropharyngeal cancer [cancer of the oropharynx, or the middle part of the throat] among men has risen more than 300 percent in the past 40 years, making oropharyngeal cancer the most common HPV-related cancer in the United States,"[9] said Ashish A. Deshmukh, a senior author of the study and an assistant professor at the University of Florida's College of Public Health and Health Professions.

Because there is no screening test for HPV in males, some people think it does not affect them. However, the truth is that they can get HPV as well as pass it on to their male or female partners.

Deshmukh offered a number of possible explanations for this stark contrast in infection rates. "One suspects the HPV persists longer ... among men and that might be causing increased prevalence. It is also possible that men acquire oral HPV more readily than women,"[10] he said. Another possibility is that females may develop greater resistance to subsequent infections once they have acquired an initial infection. Deshmukh noted that additional research is needed to fully understand the findings of the study.

CHAPTER THREE

HPV TREATMENT OPTIONS

As discussed earlier, there is currently no cure for HPV. Most infections will go away over time and will not require any treatment. However, there are treatment options available for some of the problems caused by HPV.

The two most common treatments involve surgically removing precancerous lesions in order to prevent the development of cervical cancer.

Loop electrosurgical excision procedure (LEEP) involves using a small electrical wire to excise, or remove, abnormal cells from the cervix. The procedure typically takes about 10 minutes, and while patients may feel mild discomfort or cramping, they will not feel cutting or heat from the loop. In fact, many patients do not feel anything at all.

Planned Parenthood described the basic steps a patient undergoes when having the procedure:

> You'll lie down on an exam table like you would for a Pap test. Your doctor or nurse will put a speculum into your vagina and open it. This separates the walls of your vagina so they can see your cervix.
>
> Once your doctor or nurse can see your cervix, they'll apply numbing medicine to it. Then they'll use a small tool with an electrical wire loop to remove the abnormal cells. Then your blood vessels in the area will be sealed to prevent

bleeding. They might also use a special paste called Monsel's Solution to prevent bleeding.[11]

The second most common surgical treatment for HPV is the cone biopsy, also known as cold knife conization or cold knife cone incision, which involves removing the abnormal tissue from the cervix. The term "cold knife" refers to the fact that it is performed with a surgical scalpel. This procedure is done in a hospital, and the patient is almost always given a general anesthetic, which puts them to sleep for the procedure, as opposed to a local anesthetic, which simply numbs the area the doctor is working on. Once the patient is unconscious, the doctor removes a cone-shaped sample of tissue, which is where the terms "cone biopsy," "cone incision," and "conization" come from. Typically, the patient is able to go home the same day.

Treatment Is Not a Cure

It is important to understand that removing an HPV lesion through some kind of surgical procedure is not the same as curing someone of HPV. These procedures are used only to remove the abnormal tissue caused by the virus; they do not remove the virus itself from the body. There currently is no cure for an HPV infection. After surgery, the virus generally lingers in other parts of the body. While it might go away on its own after a while, it may remain and cause additional abnormal changes. Practicing safe sex and being honest with sexual partners will continue to be important, even after treatment.

While cone biopsies are effective at removing abnormal and potentially cancerous tissue, the procedure does carry risks, such as bleeding, infection, scarring of the cervix, and cervical incompetence, which can cause difficulty getting pregnant as well as premature delivery. In contrast, the LEEP procedure generally does less damage to the cervix. LEEP also produces less bleeding and has a lower rate of post-operative infections. Still, the cone biopsy remains the preferred method in cases where the doctor suspects that some parts of a precancerous lesion lie hidden deep in the cervical tissue. In such situations, removing a large amount of tissue may be the safer approach.

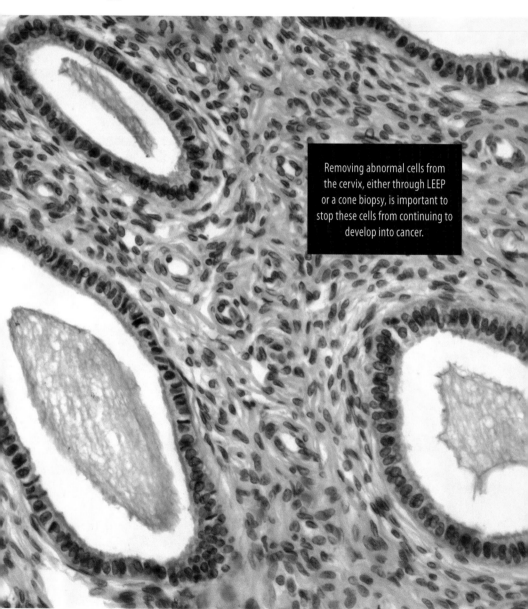

Removing abnormal cells from the cervix, either through LEEP or a cone biopsy, is important to stop these cells from continuing to develop into cancer.

Additional Treatment Options

Another common treatment option for HPV is cryotherapy, in which a doctor uses a chemical to freeze abnormal cells off the cervix. Cryotherapy can be used to remove warts and other growths from other parts of the body as well. The procedure is conducted by a doctor who uses a tool called a cryo-probe and gently holds it against the affected area for a few minutes in order to freeze the cells. The procedure generally only takes a few minutes and does not require anesthesia. After the treatment, the frozen cells thaw, and the body steadily sheds them over the course of two or three months.

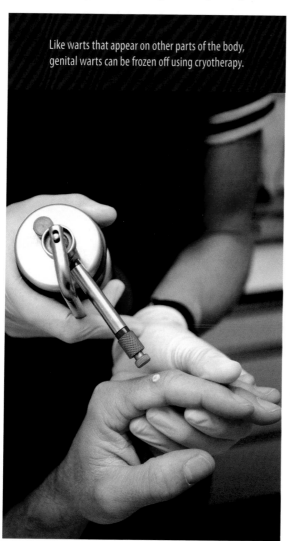

Like warts that appear on other parts of the body, genital warts can be frozen off using cryotherapy.

According to Planned Parenthood, approximately 85 to 90 percent of patients who undergo cryotherapy do not see a recurrence of the abnormal cells. However, in cases where cryotherapy does not completely remove the abnormal cells—for instance, if they are deep in the cervix—additional cryotherapy treatments may be necessary, or the doctor may recommend a different procedure, such as LEEP. Typically, cryotherapy does not affect the patient's ability to get pregnant in the future.

In contrast to cryotherapy, the doctor may choose to use laser conization to remove the cells. A laser is a device that projects a highly focused beam of light. When properly calibrated and aimed, that beam can burn away abnormal or diseased tissue. One advantage of laser therapy is that the hot beam also seals blood vessels. This results in less bleeding than in most other surgical treatments. Also, little or no scarring occurs during the healing process that follows laser therapy. Laser removal of HPV lesions generally takes place in a doctor's office with local anesthesia. As in LEEP and cone biopsies, the doctor uses a colposcope to view the cervix (or other area) during the procedure. The doctor lines up the laser precisely, then turns on the laser and zaps the cells.

Prevention Is Key for HPV

As no cure exists for HPV and treatment options currently can only address problems that occur as a result of an HPV infection, taking precautionary measures to prevent the infection in the first place is of the utmost importance.

There are a number of ways to reduce the risk of contracting HPV. As the CDC explained, "Abstaining from sexual activity is the most reliable method for preventing genital HPV infection."[12] If someone is sexually active, using latex condoms correctly and consistently can lower their chances of getting HPV, though the virus can infect areas not covered by the condom. Additionally, remaining in a long-term, mutually monogamous relationship with an uninfected partner can prevent future genital HPV infections. However, as ASHA noted, it can take weeks, months, or even years after exposure to HPV before symptoms develop or the virus is detected, so it is generally impossible to determine when or from whom HPV may have been contracted. If a person or their partner is newly diagnosed with HPV, it does not necessarily mean either of them has been unfaithful, even in a years-long relationship.

One reason keeping the risk of catching HPV within a single relationship can work is that, statistically speaking, there is a high likelihood that the virus will go away on its own in one or both partners. If that happens, that particular version of HPV will probably not return. "When an HPV infection goes away," ASHA reported, "the immune system will remember that HPV type and keep a new infection of the same HPV type from occurring again." However, ASHA continued, "Because there are many different types of HPV, becoming immune to one HPV type may not protect you from getting HPV again if exposed to another HPV type."[13] At any given time, the body's immune system targets only the specific virus it has encountered, not all HPV viruses. Thus, the partner of a person who is carrying two different HPV viruses could become infected with one or both types.

Vaccinating Against HPV

While practicing safe sex and limiting their number of sexual partners can help people prevent the spread of HPV, another key component in preventing HPV is vaccination. Vaccines are substances that, when introduced into the body, stimulate the immune system to make antibodies. These antibodies are cells that attack a particular foreign intruder, including germs associated with various diseases. The HPV vaccine prompts the immune system to attack one or more strains of the HPV virus and thereby keep the body safe from further infections by these strains. Although most people talk about "the HPV vaccine," there are actually two brands of HPV vaccine approved and licensed for use today—Gardasil and Gardasil 9. A third, called Cervarix, was available from 2007 to 2016, when its maker GlaxoSmithKline decided not to sell it in the United States anymore due to low sales.

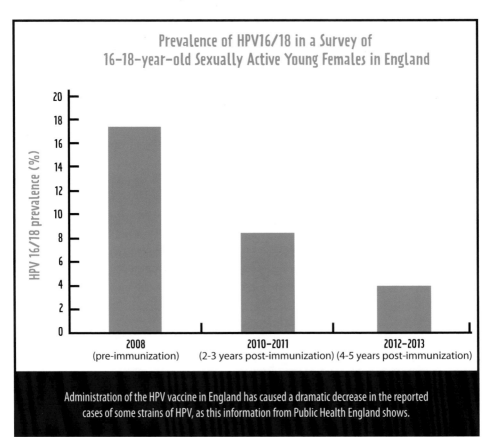

Administration of the HPV vaccine in England has caused a dramatic decrease in the reported cases of some strains of HPV, as this information from Public Health England shows.

After years of research and experiments, the Merck pharmaceutical company introduced the

Gardasil vaccine in 2006. It was licensed by the FDA that same year. It is designed to target HPV 16 and 18, which together cause approximately 70 percent of reported cases of cervical cancer. In addition, Gardasil protects against HPV 6 and 11, which cause about 90 percent of all cases of genital warts. Gardasil 9, which was approved in 2014, protects against an additional five types of HPV: types 31, 33, 45, 52, and 58, which can lead to cancer of the cervix, anus, vulva, or vagina. Because of this, the HPV vaccines are sometimes misleadingly called "cancer vaccines." It is important to note that none of these medications will treat or cure an existing HPV infection or any resulting medical issues, such as cancer. Additionally, getting vaccinated does not mean someone can never get cancer; it simply provides one line of protection against a virus that is known to cause certain types of cancer. However, even this moderate protection is a big step forward in medical science.

How Does It Work?

The HPV vaccines are made from proteins from the outer coat of certain HPV viruses. By themselves, the proteins are not complete viruses and therefore are not infectious and cannot cause disease. However, when the proteins enter the body during a vaccination, the immune system treats them as if they are complete viruses and attacks them. In the process, the body creates an immunity to these viruses.

The vaccines are given to patients in a series of intramuscular injections. For people ages 15 to 26, the vaccine is administered in three separate shots given over the course of six months. The second shot is administered two months after the first, and the third shot is given four months after the second. A recommendation from the CDC, published in December 2016, states that children ages 9 to 14 should only receive two shots, with the second shot administered six months after the first. Ideally, the vaccines should be given before the person becomes sexually active; however, if someone is eligible and sexually active, they should still be vaccinated. Vaccination after the age of 26 is less effective in lowering cancer risk.

According to a recent report from the CDC, which reviewed the data for 20,475 teenagers to estimate vaccination coverage, the vaccination rates

Medical experts recommend that children of both sexes get vaccinated against HPV to reduce their risk of developing cancer.

What About Males?

A common question doctors receive is, "Should males be vaccinated for HPV?" Males are just as likely as females to contract the virus, and they can pass it on to partners during sex or some other form of skin-to-skin contact. In fact, nearly 11 million American males have oral HPV today. The CDC currently advises that all children who are 11 or 12 years old should get the recommended series of HPV vaccine, and vaccination can start at age 9. The CDC added that the vaccine is also recommended for the following people, if they were not vaccinated as children: young men who have sex with men, including young men who identify as gay or bisexual or who intend to have sex with men through age 26; young adults who are transgender through age 26; and young adults with certain immunocompromising conditions (including HIV) through age 26.

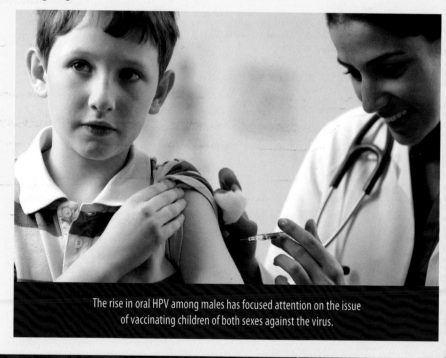

The rise in oral HPV among males has focused attention on the issue of vaccinating children of both sexes against the virus.

for HPV are rising in the United States. In 2016, 60 percent of teens ages 13 to 17 received at least one dose of the vaccine—an increase of 4 percentage points from 2015, the report stated. While these numbers are promising, there is still more work to be done to ensure all eligible individuals receive the vaccine. Only 43 percent of teens have received all the recommended doses of HPV vaccine, according to the CDC.

Debbie Saslow, PhD, senior director of HPV Related and Women's Cancers at the American Cancer Society, said, "The report shows that more US parents than ever are getting the HPV vaccine for their kids to protect them against cancer-causing infections. While the trends are positive, there is still much work to do to ensure boys and girls across the US are completing the series."[14]

Disadvantages of the HPV Vaccine

Although vaccines are a major step forward in the fight against HPV infections and HPV-related diseases, they do have certain drawbacks. First, because they do not protect against all HPV virus strains, individuals who are vaccinated can still acquire HPV infections. Therefore, females must continue to undergo regular Pap smears. Second, the vaccine may protect someone from contracting future strains of HPV, but it cannot treat existing infections. Another drawback of these vaccines is that they are expensive. According to Planned Parenthood, each dose of vaccine can cost up to $240 without insurance. Fortunately, most insurance companies cover the HPV vaccine, and there are programs to help those without insurance get vaccinated for little or no cost. For instance, the Vaccines for Children (VFC) program is federally funded and offers free injections of various vaccines to children from uninsured families as well as all Native American children. Also, many hospitals and private clinics offer free vaccination programs. Several other developed countries, including the United Kingdom, France, Canada, and Australia,

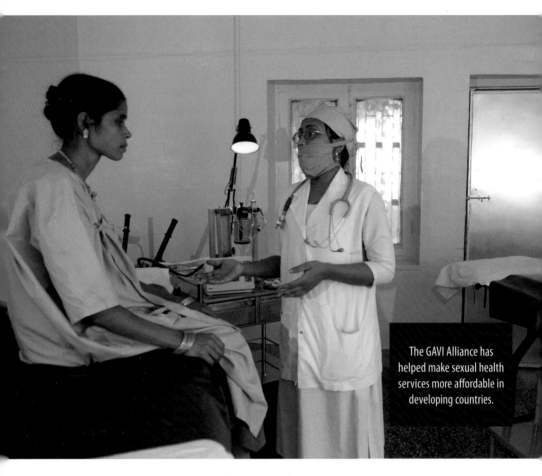

The GAVI Alliance has helped make sexual health services more affordable in developing countries.

similarly offer some free vaccination programs.

The situation is quite different for people in poorer countries, however. There, both Pap smears and HPV vaccines are far beyond the financial means of most of the population. Fortunately, though, a number of organizations are stepping in to provide much-needed funding for vaccinations in developing nations. The GAVI Alliance, which is funded by a number of governments in addition to private, corporate, and foundation donors, supports vaccination efforts all across the globe. According to a 2012 press release, the organization expects to provide vaccination for more than 30 million females in over 40 countries by the year 2020.

Controversy Surrounding the HPV Vaccine

A number of religious or conservative organizations in the United States have voiced concerns about the vaccines. The main worry is that removing much of the risk of contracting HPV might cause an increase in sexual activity among teens. According to this view, many young people refrain from having sex because they fear catching STDs, including HPV, and making the vaccines available to children will encourage them to have sex.

Many medical experts and lawmakers disagree with this view. Late in 2005, with Gardasil about to be licensed, 103 members of the U.S. House of Representatives wrote to the CDC (which advises the FDA on medical matters), urging that there be no delays in authorizing use of the vaccine. The letter stated in part,

> *Certain activists and organizations are mounting a campaign to prevent this vaccine from becoming widely available. They cite the possibility that, by preventing a horrible disease, and more than 3,700 deaths a year, this vaccine could remove an obstacle to teenage sex ... In contrast to the strong scientific evidence supporting the effectiveness of the ... vaccine, there is no scientific evidence to support the fear that its use will promote sexual activity.*[15]

Additionally, researchers have found that females vaccinated for HPV are not more likely to be sexually active. Notably, a 2012 study published in the journal *Pediatrics* found that vaccinating females for HPV at the recommended age of 11 to 12 was not associated with increased signs of sexual activity, as measured by pregnancy, STD testing or diagnosis, and contraceptive counseling.

Others have voiced concerns about the safety of the vaccine. Some parents do not want their children to be vaccinated for any disease, fearing that vaccines are dangerous; many people cite a 1998 study by Dr. Andrew Wakefield, in which Wakefield claimed he had found evidence linking vaccines and autism. However, this link has been investigated many times since then, and no evidence has been found to back up this claim. In 2004, it was revealed that Wakefield's study was funded by people who wanted a reason to sue vaccine manufacturers and that he had withheld important information that would have changed the outcome of the study; for instance, he hid the fact that some of the children who took part in the study had developmental disorders before they ever received vaccines. The paper was discredited, and Wakefield was banned from practicing medicine.

Other rumors regarding the safety of HPV vaccines have been spread as well. In 2009, the CDC's Vaccine Adverse Event Reporting System (VAERS), which monitors any negative reactions reported after someone receives a vaccine, reported that 32 women had died after receiving the Gardasil vaccine. However, it also noted that the deaths appeared to be unrelated to the vaccine, since they did not share a common pattern. VAERS only collects information; it does not analyze it to see if it is related to the vaccine. For instance, if a woman received the vaccine and then died a few weeks later from a drug overdose, that information would still be reported by VAERS as a death that occurred after receiving the vaccine. Nevertheless, many people began spreading the rumor that the vaccine could kill people. As of 2018, this rumor remains proven false but is still sometimes brought up when the safety of the vaccine is discussed. The main side effects reported from Gardasil are pain and redness where the injection was given, dizziness, nausea, headaches, and fainting, but not everyone experiences these effects.

Should Vaccination Be Mandatory?

For many Americans, though they support the availability of the vaccine, they do not support any kind of mandate or requirement to obtain the vaccine. Each state decides its own school vaccination requirements, either by the state legislature or a regulatory body such as the Board of Health. Since 2006, legislators in at least 42 states and territories have introduced legislation to require, fund, or educate the public about the HPV vaccine.

According to the National Conference of State Legislatures, "if states make the vaccine mandatory, they must also address funding issues, including for Medicaid and SCHIP [State Children's Health Insurance Program] coverage and youth who are uninsured."[16] In addition to cost, some Americans have moral objections to a mandate, or requirement, for a vaccine for an STD.

Texas became the first state to require mandatory vaccination on February 2, 2007. The state's governor at the time, Republican Rick Perry, issued an executive order, bypassing the state legislature, which required all females entering the sixth grade to receive the vaccine, with some exceptions. As reported the next day by Liz Peterson of the *Dallas Morning News*,

> *Beginning in September 2008, girls entering the sixth grade [in a Texas school]—meaning, generally, girls ages 11 and 12—will have to*

receive Gardasil, Merck & Co.'s new vaccine against strains of the human papilloma virus, or HPV. Perry also directed state health authorities to make the vaccine available free to girls 9 to 18 who are uninsured or whose insurance does not cover vaccines ... Perry, a conservative Christian ... said the cervical cancer vaccine is no different from the one that protects children against polio.[17]

Although Texas was the first state to make HPV vaccinations mandatory, it was not the last. The NCSL reported that as of March 2017, at least eight states have proposed HPV-related legislation for the 2017–2018 legislative sessions. However, when Perry announced his candidacy for president in 2011, he also announced that his decision regarding mandatory HPV vaccination had been a mistake. Although other states have proposed making the vaccine mandatory, Texas reversed that decision, proving that the debate regarding mandatory vaccination for HPV will continue into the foreseeable future.

CHAPTER FOUR

GENITAL WARTS: SYMPTOMS AND TREATMENT OPTIONS

While some strains of HPV produce no outward signs of infection, other types can cause warts—small flesh-colored bumps that often have a cauliflower-like appearance. On fingers and toes, they interrupt the fingerprint. Also known as condyloma acuminata, genital warts typically affect the moist tissues of the genital region, including the vulva, walls of the vagina, the cervix, and the anal canal in females, and the tip or shaft of the penis, the scrotum, or the anus in males. They may also arise in the mouth or throat of an individual who has engaged in oral sex with an infected person.

How Prevalent Are Genital Warts?

Prior to the HPV vaccine, approximately 340,000 to 360,000 people were treated for genital warts, according to the CDC. It is hard to determine exactly the prevalence of genital warts because many people who become infected may be unaware or too embarrassed to report it. Therefore, the CDC noted that its figures only report the number of people who sought care for genital warts. It is estimated that about 1 in 100 sexually active adults in the United States has genital warts at any given time.

The most common strains responsible for genital warts are HPV 6 and 11, which account for about 90 percent of all cases. As Planned Parenthood noted, "Genital warts are different from warts you might get elsewhere on your body. So you can't get genital warts by touching yourself (or a partner) with a wart that's on your hand or foot."[18]

Other Types of Warts

Common and plantar warts are also caused by certain strains of the HPV virus. They typically appear on the fingers or feet and can be small; grainy or rough; and white, pink, or tan in color. Often developed by children and young adults, these warts are not dangerous and spread easily through touch, either direct or indirect—for instance, via an object recently touched by someone with warts. Contrary to popular myth, they cannot be caught by touching frogs or toads. These warts generally go away on their own but can be treated with salicylic acid, cryotherapy, or laser treatment. Sometimes they have no symptoms, but other times they can make walking or holding on to things painful. Someone who has a wart should take as much care as possible not to spread it to others—for instance, if they have a wart on their finger, they should try not to shake hands with people.

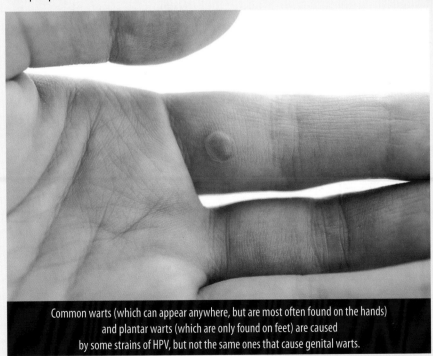

Common warts (which can appear anywhere, but are most often found on the hands) and plantar warts (which are only found on feet) are caused by some strains of HPV, but not the same ones that cause genital warts.

Diagnosing Genital Warts

It can take anywhere from a few weeks to several years after a person has sexual contact with someone who has genital warts for symptoms to arise, so knowing when they were infected and by whom can be difficult. Also, not every person exposed to genital warts will develop them. Like other strains of HPV, some people can become infected with one or more of the wart-producing types of HPV and never actually develop warts.

The reason some people merely carry these viruses is uncertain, but doctors are fairly sure that certain factors increase the risk of developing genital warts. For example, a person whose immune system is weakened is more likely to develop warts than someone whose immune system is strong. Other risk factors include cigarette smoking and poor hygiene. Studies suggest that both of these increase the likelihood that people carrying specific HPV strains will develop genital warts.

For whatever reasons people may develop condyloma, they do not always realize they have it. This is because in some situations the warts display few or no symptoms. Genital warts on the cervix, for instance, very rarely display any obvious symptoms. In contrast, warts on the vagina, vulva, penis, and some other areas sometimes display symptoms that can range from minor to very uncomfortable or even painful. These symptoms can include itching or burning sensations and minor bleeding after having sexual intercourse.

If a person starts to notice symptoms of genital warts, it is important for them to visit their doctor as soon as possible, as some of these symptoms can be signs of other—potentially more serious—health conditions. As in the case of HPV lesions, to make the diagnosis, a doctor may use a colposcope to examine the skin in one or more genital areas. Even under this device's magnification, the warts can be hard to see. Some look like very small raised bumps, not much bigger than the bumps people get on their skin when they are cold. Others are flat and can range in color from brown to almost colorless; if the warts match a person's skin tone, they can be almost invisible. In such cases, coating the area with a vinegar solution generally makes the warts stand out better.

In contrast, sometimes genital warts can be large, very unsightly bumps. They can also form thick clusters. When such a cluster of warts forms inside the urethra in the penis, it can be painful and the sufferer may have difficulty urinating. Similarly, a large cluster of genital warts in the vagina can be very uncomfortable and make it difficult for a female to have sexual intercourse. Because both small and large bumps on the skin can be something else besides genital warts, if the doctor is still unsure after the visual exam, they can order a small biopsy. The tissue sample can then be examined under a microscope to make a definite diagnosis.

Common Treatment Options

There are a number of options to treat genital warts, depending on the location and severity of the outbreak. None of the available treatments are vastly better than the others, and the same treatment may not work as well for one person as it does for another. A doctor can help their patient decide which treatment is best for them.

As with HPV in general, genital warts may go away on their own. However, they can linger, grow larger, or multiply, and they can be uncomfortable or unsightly, so patients should discuss their options with a doctor or nurse. It is important to note that any treatment option would only apply to the warts, as there is no treatment to cure the virus itself. Over-the-counter wart medicines that are sold to treat warts on the hands or feet should never be used to treat genital warts. Those chemicals are not meant to be used on the moist tissues of the genitals and can cause pain and irritation.

The most common topical medicines—medicines applied to the outside of the skin—to treat genital warts are imiquimod (sold as Aldara or Zyclara), podophyllin (sold as Podocon-25), and podofilox (sold as Condylox). Imiquimod is a cream that helps boost the immune system's ability to fight the warts. Typically, the patient will apply the cream three times a week, keeping it on for 6 to 10 hours, until the warts get smaller or disappear. However, imiquimod should not be used longer than 16 weeks, even if not all of the warts have disappeared by then. People should avoid sexual activity while the cream is on their skin, as the cream can weaken or destroy condoms and vaginal diaphragms, leading to an increased risk of unintended pregnancy or transmission of other STDs. Imiquimod can only be used on the outer skin and should not be applied in or near the eyes, lips, nostrils, vagina, or anus. The main side effect is skin redness, although it may also cause blisters, pain, cough, rashes, and fatigue.

Podofilox and podophyllin are used to destroy genital wart tissue. They both contain the same

Topical treatments are available to treat genital warts.

active ingredient, but podofilox can be applied by the patient at home, whereas a doctor must apply podophyllin. The treatment can be applied with the provided applicator, a finger, or a cotton swab. Generally, the patient applies it only to the largest, most persistent warts, and it should not be used on an area larger than 1.5 square inches (10 sq cm). The dosage, number of doses per day, and length of time someone uses the medicine will depend on where it will be used, so patients should be sure to follow all instructions from their doctor carefully to avoid any skin irritation. If the warts shrink or go away, no more treatments may be necessary. If, however, the first treatment is ineffective, it can be repeated several times for no more than four treatment cycles, taking four days off between each three-day regimen. Like imiquimod, this treatment should not be used internally. Additionally, podofilox is not recommended for use during pregnancy. Again, a doctor or nurse can advise which treatment is best for each individual.

Another common treatment for genital warts is trichloroacetic acid, or TCA, which kills the warts by destroying the proteins in the cells. This treatment is performed by a doctor or nurse and can be done in a doctor's office or clinic. TCA is safe for use internally, so vaginal, vulvar, penile, urethral, and anal warts can all be treated successfully with this approach. The physician carefully applies a small amount of the acid directly to one or more of the warts, avoiding the surrounding normal tissue that can be damaged by the solution. After the acid dries, a white, frosty-looking residue appears on the warts, a sign that the acid has destroyed part of the wart. The patient may feel heat or, occasionally, mild pain during the procedure. The typical regimen is to repeat the acid therapy once a week for up to six weeks, after which, if the warts persist, the doctor may advise trying a different approach.

In 2006, the FDA approved the use of the ointment Sinecatechins 15% (sold as Veregen) to treat genital warts. The first botanical drug ever approved for prescription use in the United States, the ointment is made from extracts of green tea leaves. Researchers are not entirely sure how the treatment works, but catechins—chemical compounds found in green tea leaves—are thought to possess antioxidant, antiviral, and antitumor properties, which can help reduce inflammation. The ointment is applied directly to the affected area by the patient three times per day for up to four months. Side effects can include redness, burning, itching, and pain where the ointment was applied. More severe reactions are rare but can include lymphadenitis, or enlargement of the lymph nodes, which are part of the body's immune system; vulvovaginitis, or an infection of the vulva and vagina; balanitis, or inflammation of the foreskin and head of the penis; and ulceration, which is the development of an open sore on the skin.

In addition to the previously described topical treatments, a doctor may advise one of several surgical options to treat genital warts. Among the more inexpensive and widely used doctor-administered treatments is cryotherapy. As in cryotherapy for HPV lesions, the procedure for warts involves using an extremely cold probe, or in many cases liquid nitrogen itself. The doctor applies the probe or nitrogen directly to the target warts. The cold kills the cells in the warts and in a small amount of surrounding skin, and after a while these cells slough off, or shed. Cryotherapy is typically performed in the doctor's office once every one to two weeks until all the warts are gone. An advantage of cryotherapy, besides its reasonable cost, is that it rarely causes any scarring. Also, it is safe to undergo during pregnancy.

Laser treatments can also be used to destroy genital warts. Most often, doctors employ a carbon dioxide laser, which vaporizes the warts. This type of treatment can be expensive, so it is generally reserved for extensive or difficult-to-treat warts.

Alternative Treatment Options

If genital warts return after initial treatment, a doctor may recommend an alternative surgical or topical treatment that, like the previously mentioned options, can be highly effective in some patients. Once again, doctors can provide guidance on the best course of treatment for individual patients.

The first of these alternative treatments is surgical incision, or the cutting away of the wart or warts. Although this treatment is now considered outdated, it is still effective and often preferred for treating large lesions that either require immediate intervention or have proven to be unresponsive to less drastic measures. Surgical excision has a clearance rate of about 72 percent. Mohs surgery, a microscopically controlled procedure that is typically used to treat carcinomas, or cancers, on the skin, has become a popular option for surgical excision of warts. This technique allows the doctor to more precisely remove just the affected tissue, leaving the surrounding healthy tissue intact.

Another surgical procedure for treating condyloma is electrosurgery, an extremely effective short-term solution that involves using high-frequency electrical currents to burn and destroy warty lesions. It is especially effective for small warts on the shaft of the penis, the rectum, or the vulva. However, it can cause irreversible damage to the surrounding tissues, and the patient is often under general anesthesia, which comes with more risks than local anesthesia. After the anesthesia wears off, these may include headache, nausea and vomiting, dizziness, and vision problems. Most of these are temporary but unpleasant. Additionally, some people with other health problems are not able to undergo general anesthesia; for instance, in some people, it can increase the risk of stroke or heart attack. For these reasons, electrosurgery can be an impractical option for many.

How to Avoid Spreading Genital Warts

Planned Parenthood advises the following ways to reduce the risk of spreading and catching genital warts:

- *Encourage your partner to talk with a doctor or nurse about the HPV vaccine. Most brands can protect against some types of the virus that cause most cases of genital warts.*

- *Always use condoms and dental dams during oral, anal, and vaginal sex.*

- *Don't have sex when you have visible warts, even with a condom. There may be warts on places the condom doesn't cover.*

- *Stop smoking. If you smoke, you may have a bigger chance of getting warts than people who don't smoke, and warts are more likely to come back if you smoke.*

- *Always tell your sexual partners that you have genital warts before you have sex so you can work together to prevent them from spreading.*[1]

1. "How Can I Prevent Getting or Spreading Genital Warts?," Planned Parenthood, accessed December 11, 2017. www.plannedparenthood.org/learn/stds-hiv-safer-sex/genital-warts/how-can-i-prevent-getting-or-spreading-genital-warts.

Post-Treatment Tips

Many people wonder if there is anything they can do after undergoing treatment for genital warts to prevent them from coming back. Unfortunately, the answer is no. According to Planned Parenthood,

Genital warts can be treated, but they can't be cured. You're removing the warts, but you'll still have the virus that causes them. The virus may go away at some point on its own, but

there's no way to know for sure. Some people will get warts again and others won't.

The best actions you can take after undergoing wart removal treatment is to keep the area clean and avoid scratching it. Also, be sure to wash your hands after touching the area where the warts were, and avoid sex if it's uncomfortable.[19]

CHAPTER FIVE

HPV-RELATED CANCERS

Without a doubt, the consequence of an HPV infection most likely to cause fear and anxiety in patients is the development of some form of cancer. It can take years, even decades, after infection occurs for HPV to develop into cancer, and there is no way to know whether a person with HPV will eventually develop health complications. That is why it is incredibly important to receive regular Pap smears and other routine screenings, as recommended by a doctor, to identify problems before they can become more dangerous.

Cervical cancer is one of the most common cancer types caused by the HPV virus. In fact, HPV is responsible for about 90 percent of all cases of cervical cancer. However, the virus has been linked to a number of other types of cancer, including vaginal cancer, cancer of the vulva, penile cancer, anal cancer, oral cancer, and more.

To understand how cancers spread and how doctors attempt to treat them, it is important to understand what cancer is. A cancer is made up of groups of abnormal cells that appear inside the body and proceed to multiply. Most of the body's cells multiply by dividing in half from time to time, thereby creating new, healthy tissues while shedding older cells. For example, about once a month, new bodily skin cells form and older ones fall away. In a manner that is still not well understood, the body tells these healthy cells that it is time to divide and also signals them when it is time to stop dividing.

In people with cancer, this normal process of new cell creation is disrupted. Again for reasons that are somewhat uncertain, cells in one spot in the body do not receive the "stop dividing" signal aimed at them, so they continue to divide and multiply. Over the course of days, weeks, and months, they form a cluster, called a tumor. The tumor often gets bigger and bigger until it begins to press on surrounding nerves, causing pain; up until this point, there may not be any symptoms. If the abnormal cells multiply very slowly and

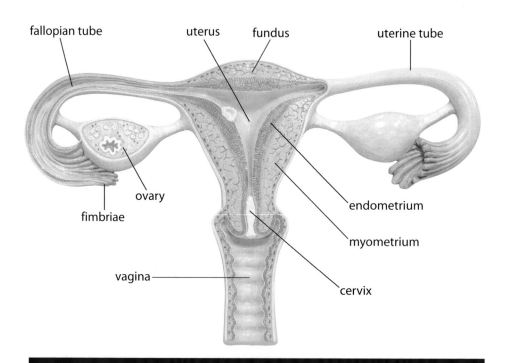

There are many different cancers that can affect the female reproductive system, which is shown here.

are harmless to the body, the tumor is said to be benign. However, if the abnormal cells continue to multiply and prove harmful to the body, the tumor is said to be malignant. Malignant tumors sometimes spread beyond the initial location of the tumor and invade other parts of the body, a process called metastasis. For example, cervical cancer caused by HPV can metastasize into the bladder, rectum, or even the lungs and liver. However, cancers are still referred to by their starting point; for example, cervical cancer that has spread to the bladder is called metastatic cervical cancer, not bladder cancer.

Cancer of the Vulva

Vulvar cancer affects the vulva—the area located just outside the vagina and containing the labia (vaginal lips) and clitoris. As of 2018, it accounts for about 6 percent of cancers of the female reproductive organs and 0.7 percent of all cancer in females. In 2017, the American Cancer Society (ACS) estimated that about 6,190 cancers of the vulva would be diagnosed in 2018 and that about 1,200 females would die of this cancer. It typically affects the inner edges of the labia, though it can occasionally occur on the clitoris or in the Bartholin glands, which are located just inside the opening of the vagina and are responsible for keeping the vagina moist. Symptoms can include itching, a burning sensation, or small white bumps on the vulva. To diagnose vulvar cancer, a doctor will perform a pelvic exam and possibly a Pap smear. The only way to confirm that cancer is present is through a biopsy. Typical treatments include surgical incision in the early stages and radiation therapy or chemotherapy in more advanced stages.

Cancer of the Cervix

Cervical cancer is the most common HPV-related cancer. Incidence rates are higher worldwide than in the United States, though, which may be due to the widespread use of preventive screenings in American society. Nevertheless, the incidence of cervical cancer in the United States is still worrisome and tragic. In 2014, around 12,500 American females were diagnosed with cervical cancer, and just over 4,000 died from the disease.

Cervical cancer is most often caused by HPV 16 and 18, but others, including HPV 31, 33, 42, 42, and 58, can also cause it. Whichever virus strain is involved, its presence is frequently not the only factor in the development of the disease. Other factors that increase the risk of contracting cervical cancer include a family history of the disease, being a smoker, having many sexual partners, having an existing HIV infection, poor diet, long-term use of oral contraceptives, and multiple pregnancies.

Once HPV—aided by one or more of these other factors—has caused the development of a cancerous tumor, there are often no symptoms, at least in the early stages of the cancer. Symptoms of more advanced cervical cancer include vaginal bleeding; a watery, bloody discharge from the vagina that may have a foul odor; and pain during sexual intercourse.

According to the American Cancer Society, cervical cancer typically starts in the cells lining the cervix. These cells gradually develop pre-cancerous changes, which eventually turn into cancer. The ACS continued, "Although cervical cancers start from cells with pre-cancerous changes (pre-cancers), only some women with

Birth Control and Cervical Cancer

Females who use an intrauterine device (IUD) may have a lower risk of developing cervical cancer, according to a recent study published in the journal *Obstetrics & Gynecology*. In the study, researchers found the rate of cervical cancer was one-third lower in females who used an IUD (a device used to prevent pregnancy) than in those who did not. Although the researchers did not investigate exactly how the device could have this effect, they hypothesize that the device may trigger an immune response that effectively targets and destroys HPV. Further research is needed to determine the mechanism by which this popular birth control method may impact cervical cancer risk, but the study's researchers were hopeful that IUDs could have a strong impact on populations with less access to preventative health services, such as HPV vaccination and cancer screenings.

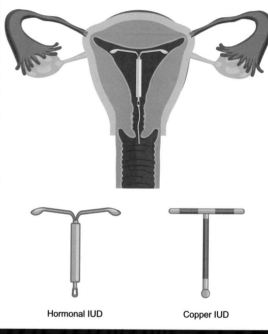

Intrauterine Device (IUD)

Hormonal IUD   Copper IUD

Researchers believe IUDs may offer some protection against cervical cancer, but more study is necessary to fully understand this connection.

pre-cancers of the cervix will develop cancer. It usually takes several years for cervical pre-cancer to change to cervical cancer, but it can happen in less than a year."[20]

Once a diagnosis of cervical cancer has been confirmed, further tests are conducted to determine the stage of the disease, which describes its size, how far it has grown in the cervix, and whether it has metastasized. Determining the stage of the disease helps guide the course of treatment. In general, stage 1 means the cancer is confined to the cervix itself. In stage 2, the cancer is present in the cervix and the upper portion of the vagina. Stage 3 describes cases in which the cancer extends as far as the lower portion of the vagina or internally to the pelvic side wall. In stage 4, the cancer has spread to nearby organs, such as the bladder or rectum, or it has spread to other areas of the body.

To determine which of these stages of cervical cancer exists in a patient, a doctor goes through many of the same steps they would use to diagnose HPV lesions. Close inspection of the cervix with a colposcope occurs, often followed by a biopsy, after which a pathologist examines the excised tissue and looks for cancerous cells. In cases in which the cancer appears to be quite advanced, other diagnostic tests may be called for. Imaging tests, such as X-rays, computerized tomography (CT) scans, and magnetic resonance imaging (MRI) help determine whether the cancer has spread beyond the cervix. A CT puts together many X-rays to form a more detailed image, and an MRI uses a magnetic field and sound waves to create a computerized image. With the help of these tests, doctors can get a clearer picture of the body.

The course of treatment for cervical cancer depends on several factors, including the stage of the cancer, the patient's overall health, and their preferences. If someone is diagnosed with cervical cancer, their doctor can discuss all the options and help them decide which treatment is right. Most people who have cancer see a cancer specialist called an oncologist in addition to their regular doctor. Treatment options include surgery, radiation, chemotherapy, or a combination of the three.

Cryosurgery, laser surgery, LEEP, and cold knife conization are treatments for stage 0 cancer, or precancer. Beginning in stage 1, the treatment options start to vary depending on whether the patient wants to continue to be able to have children and whether the cancer has spread to the blood or lymphovascular system.

In mild stage 1 cases, for instance, in which the tumor is small and very localized, simple surgical excision—a cone biopsy—may be all that is required. The doctor cuts away the abnormal

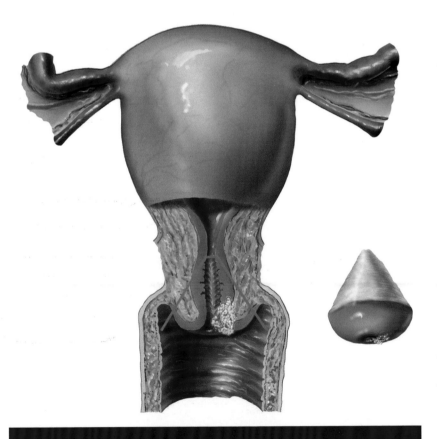

If cervical cancer is caught early enough, a cone biopsy (shown here) may be enough to remove it.

tissue plus, for safety, some of the normal tissue surrounding it. Follow-up includes continued Pap smears and frequent checkups in the doctor's office to be sure that the cancer has not returned.

In many cases, however, the cancer has spread too far for a local surgical excision to be successful. The next step, assuming the cancer has not spread beyond the cervix, is a radical trachelectomy—also called a cervicectomy—meaning removal of the entire cervix. The benefit of this treatment is it allows many cervical cancer survivors to keep their uterus, which means they have a chance to become pregnant later.

This is unfortunately not the case with patients whose cervical cancer has spread beyond the cervix. In such cases, the doctor most often advises a hysterosalpingo-oophorectomy. In this major operation, the cervix, uterus, and fallopian tubes (through which eggs from the ovaries reach the uterus) are all removed, so pregnancy is no longer an option. When this is done on patients over age 40, the ovaries are frequently removed, too. When they consider it to be necessary, doctors also remove the lymph nodes surrounding the area.

Additional Treatment Options for Cervical Cancer

Radiation therapy, which uses high-powered energy beams, can be used alone or in addition to chemotherapy, before or after surgery, to either shrink or kill tumor cells. The radiation kills the cancer cells, prevents them from further dividing, or does both.

Two general kinds of radiation therapy are used to treat cervical cancer: external beam radiation therapy (EBRT) and brachytherapy, which is an internal procedure. The terms "internal" and "external" identify whether the treatment is given inside or outside the body. The American Cancer Society describes EBRT as "like getting a regular X-ray, but the radiation dose is stronger."[21] Each EBRT treatment takes only a few minutes, and the procedure is painless. Following these treatments, patients often feel tired and may experience upset stomach, diarrhea, nausea, and vomiting. Also, they may experience patches of dry skin in the treated area, which may also feel itchy or hard; vaginal pain; and menstrual changes.

Brachytherapy involves putting the radiation source in or near the cancer. While the patient is under either local or general anesthetic, a thin tube is inserted into the vagina and placed up against the affected region of the cervix. Low-dose rate brachytherapy is conducted over a few days, with the patient remaining in the hospital and instruments holding the radiation in place. High-dose rate brachytherapy is an outpatient procedure conducted over several weeks. "Outpatient" means the person comes to the hospital for treatments but goes home in between. In this case, the radioactive material is inserted for a few minutes and then removed. The most common side effect of this type of treatment is vaginal irritation. It may also cause similar symptoms to EBRT.

Chemotherapy, which uses powerful drugs to fight the cancer, is sometimes used together with radiation therapy. The drugs are mostly either injected with a needle, administered through an IV tube, or taken by mouth. When they are used together, chemotherapy and radiation therapy can be considerably more effective than when only one is used. However, chemotherapy has a number of very unpleasant side effects, including nausea, vomiting, kidney damage, hair loss, and damage to the immune system. So both doctor and patient must carefully weigh the benefits and drawbacks of choosing chemotherapy, whether it is used alone or along with radiation therapy.

Thankfully, the HPV vaccines have been proven to be very effective in reducing the incidence of cervical cancers. According to a CDC study published in the journal *Pediatrics*, the HPV vaccine has helped reduce the prevalence of cervical cancer by 64 percent in females aged 14 to 19 years and by 34 percent among those aged 20 to 24 years. The hope, of course, is that widespread vaccination can vastly reduce the number of lives lost to cervical cancer as well as other HPV-related cancers.

Cancer of the Vagina

Fortunately, vaginal cancer is rare, compared to cervical cancer, with only one of every 1,100 females developing the disease in her lifetime. The American Cancer Society estimated that in 2018, about 5,170 new cases of vaginal cancer would be diagnosed and about 1,330 females would die from the disease. Approximately 70 percent of vaginal cancers begin growing in the squamous cells of the vagina and develop slowly over many years. Squamous cells "are thin, flat cells that look like fish scales;"[22] they are a type of skin cell that can be found in the lining of the vagina. Other types of vaginal cancer affect other types of cells; for instance, vaginal sarcoma, which is more rare, affects connective tissue. Patients in the early stages of vaginal cancer may not experience any symptoms, but as the disease progresses, patients may experience vaginal bleeding (after intercourse or after menopause), a watery discharge, painful or frequent urination, constipation, pelvic pain, or a lump in the vagina.

Treatments for vaginal cancers are similar to some of those used to deal with cervical cancer. Small tumors or lesions may be surgically removed, or a doctor may recommend removing part of the vagina, depending on the extent of the cancer. Most vaginal cancer patients also undergo EBRT.

If the radiation therapy fails to destroy all the cancer, more extreme measures may be necessary to save the patient's life. If the cancer has spread beyond the vagina, a hysterectomy (removal of just the uterus) or hysterosalpingo-oophorectomy is generally performed. Chemotherapy, in combination with radiation, also may be used to treat more advanced stages of the disease. In the most extreme cases, in which the cancer keeps coming back, it might be necessary to remove the majority of the pelvic organs, a procedure known as pelvic exenteration.

Cancer of the Penis

Penile cancer is far more rare in North America and Europe than it is in some parts of Asia, Africa, and South America. According to the American Cancer Society, penile cancer accounts for less than 1 percent of cancers in males in the United States. It estimated that in 2018, about 2,320 new cases of penile cancer would be diagnosed and about 380 males would die from the disease. Studies have shown that uncircumcised males have a higher risk of contracting HPV infections, penile dysplasia, and penile cancer. This is because these problems most often occur under the foreskin, where poor hygiene increases their likelihood. A circumcised male does not have foreskin because it is removed when he is a baby.

Penile cancer is typically treated through surgery,

with radiation therapy used either instead of or in addition to surgery. When penile cancer is caught in its early stages, a small biopsy (sometimes called microsurgery) may be enough to remove it. If the male is uncircumcised, the doctor may also remove the foreskin. This lowers the risk of recurrence. If the cancer has spread, chemotherapy may be given. If the cancer cannot be cured by other means, a partial or complete penectomy, or removal of the penis, is performed. Plastic surgery can reconstruct the penis, allowing the patient to urinate normally.

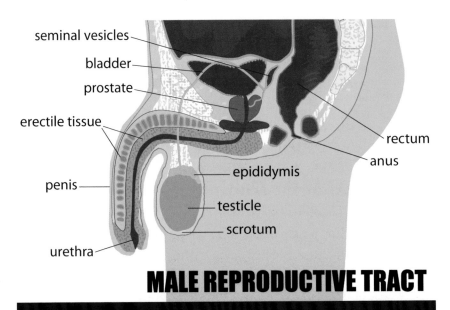

seminal vesicles

bladder

prostate

erectile tissue

rectum

anus

epididymis

penis

testicle

scrotum

urethra

MALE REPRODUCTIVE TRACT

HVP can lead to penile cancer in males. Shown here is a diagram of the male reproductive system.

Cancer of the Anus

Another rare form of cancer associated with HPV infection is anal cancer. It was estimated that about 8,580 new cases of anal cancer would be diagnosed in 2018 and about 1,160 people would die of the disease. Anal cancer is most often associated with HPV 16 and 18, the same two that cause a majority of

Raising Awareness for HPV-Linked Oral Cancer

In August 2010, actor Michael Douglas was diagnosed with stage 4 oral cancer. Though many assumed the disease was related to years of tobacco and alcohol use, the actor later revealed that his cancer may have been linked to an HPV infection. In an interview with the *Guardian*, a British newspaper, the actor said, "I did worry if the stress by my son's incarceration [stay in prison] didn't help trigger it. But yeah, it's a sexually transmitted disease that causes cancer."[1] Douglas underwent an intensive eight-week course of chemotherapy and radiation, which was successful in treating his cancer. Currently, the CDC recommends all children ages 11 to 12, regardless of gender, receive an HPV vaccine to help prevent the development of cancers associated with HPV.

Actor Michael Douglas has stated that HPV may have been the cause of his oral cancer. This has raised awareness of this issue among the general public.

1. Quoted in Catherine Shoard, "Michael Douglas: Oral Sex Caused My Cancer," *Guardian*, June 2, 2013. www.theguardian.com/film/2013/jun/02/michael-douglas-oral-sex-cancer.

cervical cancers. This means that a patient with cervical dysplasia or cervical cancer is at risk for anal cancer, too. The risk of anal cancer is also higher for people who engage in certain behaviors, notably smoking, having multiple sex partners, and engaging in anal intercourse.

The symptoms of anal cancer can be somewhat different than for most other cancers caused by HPV, although diagnosis and treatment are generally the same. Rectal bleeding is often the first sign of anal cancer. Other symptoms can include rectal itching, a lump at the anus, pain or a feeling of fullness in the area, abnormal discharge, and changes in bowel movements. The American Cancer Society added,

> *Most often these types of symptoms are more likely to be caused by benign (non-cancerous) conditions, like hemorrhoids, anal fissures, or anal warts. Still, if you have any of these symptoms, it's important to have them checked by a doctor so that the cause can be found and treated, if needed.*[23]

Diagnosis of anal cancer is generally done through physical examination, ultrasound of the anal canal, and tissue biopsy. An ultrasound is "an examination using high-frequency sound waves to create images of tissue layers beneath the surface."[24] Most people are familiar with ultrasounds done on pregnant women to get a picture of the baby, but ultrasounds can be used the same way on other parts of the body. The most common treatment is a combination of chemotherapy and radiation therapy. Radiation treatment typically takes five to six weeks, with chemotherapy being administered during the first and fifth weeks. Surgery may also be used to remove small tumors during early stages of the disease. If the disease is far advanced or has not responded to chemotherapy and radiation, an abdominoperineal resection may be recommended. According to the Mayo Clinic, "During this procedure the surgeon removes the anal canal, rectum, and a portion of the colon. The surgeon then attaches the remaining portion of your colon to an opening (stoma) in your abdomen through which waste will leave your body and collect in a colostomy bag."[25]

Oral Cancer

HPV-related oral cancer also poses a risk to people everywhere, though it is more than twice as common in males as in females. The American Cancer Society estimated that about 49,670 people would be diagnosed with oral cavity or oropharyngeal cancer in 2017, with an estimated 9,700 dying from the disease. Oral cancer was generally linked with alcohol and tobacco use in past generations, but rates of the disease have remained about the same in recent decades, despite falling rates of smoking. Recent studies have shown an alarming increase in the number of oral cancers caused by HPV 16 and, to a lesser extent, other HPV types. These viruses may now account for as many as 25 to 35 percent of all oral cancer cases. Medical authorities say that most often the viruses spread from the genital region to the mouth during oral sex. Surgical excision, radiation therapy, and chemotherapy are all used to treat oral cancer. Unfortunately, there is currently no test that can be done to see whether someone has HPV in the mouth or throat.

CHAPTER SIX

THE EMOTIONAL IMPACT OF HPV

Receiving a diagnosis of HPV, or any STD for that matter, can be distressing. The person might be unfamiliar with the infection, or they may be concerned about long-term health consequences and how the diagnosis may affect their current or future romantic relationships. These are all valid feelings.

There is a certain stigma, or negative view, attached to STDs, which can make a person who is diagnosed with one feel ashamed. STDs are very common; according to Dr. Lois Ramondetta, chief of gynecologic oncology at the MD Anderson Cancer Center in Houston, "almost every human being is going to get HPV at some point in their life through normal, intimate human activity."[26] Despite this, there is still a lot of shame surrounding an STD diagnosis. Jenelle Marie Pierce, founder and executive director of The STD Project, calls this "scarlet-lettering." She wrote, "The rules surrounding sex and all things 'coupling' have become so brazenly ambiguous these days—that is, until you catch an STD. At which point, you are [seen as] a sinner, dirty, damaged goods, and you will, hence forth, pay for your bad behavior."[27] In other words, more people are tolerant of sexual activity outside of marriage than they were in the past, but attitudes toward STDs have still not changed much.

Millions of Americans at any given time are infected with an STD, and yet the stigma persists that contracting an infectious disease as a result of sexual activity indicates a moral or ethical failure. This is a false equivalency, which does nothing but make people feel guilty and keep others from getting regular screenings out of fear for what they may find.

What can be done about it? Pierce offered the following advice to help eradicate the stigma surrounding STDs:

- *Add "people with STDs" to your mental list of groups facing discrimination.*

- *Pay attention to metaphors like "dirty" and "damaged goods" and stop using them.*

- *Pay attention to stereotypes. Correct people when they try to say that being a slut means you probably have an STI/STD.*

- *Tell your story—let others know they are not alone.*[28]

Coping with a Diagnosis

Although HPV is very common, its serious, long-term health consequences mean it is reasonable to be worried about getting that diagnosis. Indeed, getting any STD diagnosis can feel unpleasant. As with any stressful situation, self-care is incredibly important following an STD diagnosis.

Kristen Sollee of *Bustle* offered the following six ways to cope with an STD diagnosis:

1. ***Allow Yourself to React.*** *Sometimes a diagnosis can be devastating for a multitude of reasons, and you should give yourself*

time to grieve before even trying to get your [stuff] together.

2. **Don't Slut-Shame Yourself.** *You don't need to have sex with more than one person to contract an STD, and it doesn't mean you're a "slut" (whatever that word even means) if you do contract one. The worst thing you can do is beat yourself up over the sexual circumstances that led to your diagnosis.*

3. **Talk to an Expert.** *Don't freak out on WebMD before talking to your GP or a specialist about your diagnosis.*

4. **Talk to Someone You Love.** *Choose a close friend or family member to disclose your diagnosis to who won't slut-shame or judge you. Emotional support can help you make informed choices, and it's way easier than going it alone.*

5. **Notify Your Partners.** *This is a tough one. It's definitely not pleasant to have to call, text, or tell someone in person that you have an STD, but it's pretty important that you do. If you fear for your safety or just absolutely can't stomach passing on this pertinent info, inSPOT is a service that can notify someone anonymously that they should get tested.*

6. **Know You Are Not Your Diagnosis.** *Just because you have an STD doesn't mean it has to define you—even if you contract something chronic like HIV, HPV, or herpes. Although that's way easier said than done, particularly in the beginning, there are many, many cases of people living healthy, rewarding lives despite their diagnosis.*[29]

It is normal to feel upset or scared after receiving a diagnosis of HPV. Proper self-care involves not ignoring those feelings.

Talking to a Partner About Safe Sex

Preventative measures against HPV, such as vaccination and getting regular routine screenings, are important actions people can take to avoid some of its adverse consequences. However, the best way for individuals to prevent infection is by taking control of their health and avoiding risky behaviors, such as engaging in unprotected sex and having multiple sex partners. Speaking openly and honestly with a partner about sex is immensely important for both physical and emotion health. Ideally, people would discuss both partners' STD status, their preferred method of protection, and relationship exclusivity before they start having sex with a new partner.

Notifying a Partner

Many people are scared to tell a partner that they have an STD. Some are afraid their partner will judge them or be angry, while others are concerned people will no longer want to have sex with them. However, part of having responsible sex means having these types of conversations. Talking about STDs openly helps fight the stigma surrounding them. In some cases, having an honest, open conversation about the reality of HPV helps correct people's misconceptions about the disease and lead to less judgment. Additionally, hiding important information from a current or potential sexual partner takes away their right to make their own decisions about their body. Planned Parenthood offered some tips to help people have this tough conversation:

- "Keep calm and carry on. Lots of people have genital warts, and plenty of them are in relationships. For most couples, having genital warts isn't a huge deal. Try to go into the conversation with a calm, positive attitude. Having genital warts is simply a health issue—it doesn't say anything about you as a person."[1]

- Pick a time when both partners are calm and undistracted. Pick a place that feels safe, relaxed, and private.

- Practice what to say ahead of time, possibly with a friend.

- "Make it a two-way conversation. Remember that STDs are super common, so who knows? Your partner might have genital warts, too. So start by asking if they've ever been tested or if they've had an STD before."[2]

- Come prepared with accurate facts to counter any misperceptions the other person may have.

- If the relationship is abusive and the person is afraid their partner may physically hurt them, it may be safer to tell them through e-mail or text.

1. "How Can I Prevent Getting or Spreading Genital Warts?," Planned Parenthood, accessed December 11, 2017. www.plannedparenthood.org/learn/stds-hiv-safer-sex/genital-warts/how-can-i-prevent-getting-or-spreading-genital-warts.

2. "How Can I Prevent Getting or Spreading Genital Warts?," Planned Parenthood.

Talking to a partner about sex can feel uncomfortable at first, but people's health and happiness are much more important than a few minutes of embarrassment. A person who values their partner's health will listen and participate in the conversation even if they find it uncomfortable. Anyone who refuses to discuss safe sex, gets angry when the topic is brought up, or insists that it does not apply to them is putting their health and their partner's health at risk. Planned Parenthood offered the following guidance on how to start a conversation about safe sex with a new partner:

> *The best time to talk about your safer sex game plan is BEFORE you start having sex (including oral sex). Make sure you're both cool with using condoms and/or [dental] dams to protect yourselves, and figure out when and how you're going to get tested for STDs. Some good questions to ask someone before having sex with them include:*
>
> - *Do you know if you have any STDs?*
> - *When was the last time you were tested for STDs?*
> - *Do you usually use condoms and/or dental dams?*
> - *Have you ever shared needles with someone for tattoos, piercings, or shooting drugs?*
> - *Have you had any STDs before? Which ones? Did you get them treated?*
>
> *It's totally normal to be embarrassed at first, but you'll feel better once you get it over with. And your partner will probably be glad you brought it up. A good way to start is by telling your partner that you care about them and want to do everything you can to make sure you're protecting them and the relationship.*

You can also talk about your own safe sex history first, which might make your partner feel more comfortable opening up. It's also a great idea to suggest that you get tested together so you can support each other.[30]

Talking to a new sexual partner about safe sex may feel uncomfortable, but it is an essential part of having a healthy sex life.

Preventing the spread of HPV begins with individuals. By knowing the facts and taking good care of themselves, including getting vaccinated, receiving regular screenings, and practicing safe sex, people can greatly reduce their risk of contracting HPV and thereby avoid its consequences. Be your own best friend. You know you would never let your best friend do anything that would put them in danger, and if they were experiencing unusual health symptoms, you would encourage them to see a doctor. Apply that same concern to yourself. Be smart about your health, be honest with your partners, and, most importantly, be kind to yourself.

Chapter One:
The Truth About HPV

1. Karen, interview by Don Nardo, 2007.

2. Karen, interview.

3. "HPV: Myths and Facts," American Sexual Health Association. www.ashasexualhealth. org/stdsstis/hpv/hpv-myths-facts/.

4. Gregory S. Henderson et al., *Women at Risk: The HPV Epidemic and Your Cervical Health.* New York, NY: Penguin, 2002, p. 40.

Chapter Two:
Detecting HPV Infections

5. Henderson et al., *Women at Risk*, p. 54.

6. Mayo Clinic Staff, "Pap Smear," Mayo Clinic, June 11, 2015. www.mayoclinic.org/ tests-procedures/pap-smear/basics/results/prc-20013038.

7. "What's a Pap Test?," Planned Parenthood, November 4, 2017. www.plannedparenthood. org/learn/cancer/cervical-cancer/whats-pap-test.

8. "2015 Sexually Transmitted Diseases Treatment Guidelines: HPV-Associated Cancers and Precancers," CDC, last updated January 25, 2017. www.cdc.gov/std/tg2015/hpv-cancer.htm.

9. Quoted in Susan Scutti, "One in Nine American Men Has Oral HPV, Study Finds," CNN, October 16, 2017. www.cnn.com/2017/10/16/

health/oral-hpv-infections-men-study/index.
html.

10. Quoted in Scutti, "One in Nine American Men
Has Oral HPV, Study Finds."

Chapter Three:
HPV Treatment Options

11. "What's LEEP?," Planned Parenthood, November 5, 2017. www.plannedparenthood.org/
learn/cancer/cervical-cancer/whats-leep.

12. "2015 Sexually Transmitted Diseases Treatment Guidelines," CDC.

13. "HPV & Relationships," American Sexual Health Association, November 5, 2017.
www.ashasexualhealth.org/stdsstis/hpv/
hpv-relationships/.

14. Quoted in Stacy Simon, "HPV Vaccination
Rates Are Rising Among American Teens,"
American Cancer Society, August 24, 2017.
www.cancer.org/latest-news/hpv-vaccination-
rates-are-rising-among-american-teens.html.

15. Quoted in Nancy Gibb, "Defusing the War
over the 'Promiscuity' Vaccine," *TIME*,
June 21, 2006. www.time.com/time/nation/
article/0,8599,1206813,00.html.

16. "HPV Vaccine: State Legislation and Statutes,"
National Conference of State Legislatures,
July 10, 2017. www.ncsl.org/research/health/
hpv-vaccine-state-legislation-and-statutes.
aspx.

17. Liz Peterson, "Texas Governor Orders
Anti-Cancer Vaccine for School Girls," *Dallas
Morning News*, February 3, 2007. www.dallas-
news.com/sharedcontent/APStories/stories/
D8N1TCI80.html.

Chapter Four:
Genital Warts: Symptoms and Treatment Options

18. "Genital Warts," Planned Parenthood, November 11, 2017. www.plannedparenthood. org/learn/stds-hiv-safer-sex/genital-warts.

19. "How Do I Get Treated for Genital Warts?," Planned Parenthood, November 11, 2017. www.plannedparenthood.org/learn/stds-hiv-safer-sex/genital-warts/how-do-i-get-treated-genital-warts.

Chapter Five:
HPV-Related Cancers

20. "What Is Cervical Cancer?," American Cancer Society, last updated December 9, 2016. www.cancer.org/cancer/cervical-cancer/prevention-and-early-detection/what-is-cervical-cancer.html.

21. "Radiation Therapy for Cervical Cancer," American Cancer Society, December 5, 2016. www.cancer.org/cancer/cervical-cancer/treating/radiation.html.

22. "Squamous Cell Carcinoma," NCI Dictionary of Cancer Terms, National Cancer Institute, accessed December 12, 2017. www.cancer.gov/publications/dictionaries/cancer-terms?cdrid=46595.

23. "Signs and Symptoms of Anal Cancer," American Cancer Society, January 20, 2016. www.cancer.org/cancer/anal-cancer/detection-diagnosis-staging/signs-and-symptoms.html.

24. "Rectal Ultrasound," Colon & Rectal Surgery Associates, accessed December 12, 2017.

www.colonrectal.org/services.cfm/sid:6695/
Rectal_Ultrasound/index.html.

25. "Anal Cancer: Diagnosis & Treatment,"
    Mayo Clinic, August 18, 2017. www.
    mayoclinic.org/diseases-conditions/anal-
    cancer/diagnosis-treatment/drc-20354146.

Chapter Six:
The Emotional Impact of HPV

26. Quoted in Maggi Fox, "HPV Is Spread by
    Having Sex. So Why Don't People Talk
    About That?," NBC News, October 23, 2017.
    www.nbcnews.com/health/health-news/hpv-
    spread-having-sex-so-why-don-t-people-
    talk-n812421.

27. Jenelle Marie Pierce, "STD Stigma—The New
    Scarlet Letter," The STD Project, November
    18, 2017. www.thestdproject.com/stds-scarlet-
    letter-std-stigma/.

28. Pierce, "STD Stigma."

29. Sollee, Kristen, "6 Ways to Cope with an
    STD Diagnosis," *Bustle*, November 20, 2015.
    www.bustle.com/articles/125157-6-ways-to-
    cope-with-an-std-diagnosis.

30. "How Do I Talk to My Partner About Saf-
    er Sex?," Planned Parenthood, November 12,
    2017. www.plannedparenthood.org/learn/stds-
    hiv-safer-sex/safer-sex/how-do-i-talk-my-
    partner-about-safer-sex.

basal cells: Cells located in the lower portion of bodily tissues; basal cells regularly divide, creating new cells.

Bethesda Classification System: A comprehensive system used by doctors to classify the results of a Pap smear, including any abnormalities that are identified through the test.

biopsy: The surgical removal of a small amount of bodily tissue, either for diagnostic purposes or as treatment.

cervix: The lower, narrow portion of the uterus, leading into the vagina.

colposcope: A device equipped with a magnifying lens, used by doctors to examine the surface of the skin; the procedure in which a colposcope is used is called a colposcopy.

condyloma acuminata: The medical name for genital warts.

cryotherapy: A medical treatment that uses extreme cold to freeze and destroy abnormal or diseased bodily tissue.

dysplasia: An area of abnormal cells.

electrosurgery: A surgical procedure in which genital or other warts are burned away by an electrical current.

gender identity: A person's innermost concept of self, either as a man, a woman, a blend of both, or neither. One's gender identity can be the same as or different than their sex assigned at birth.

imiquimod: A topical cream generally applied by patients to treat their genital warts.

laryngeal papillomatosis: HPV-related warts or other growths that form in the throat, specifically the larynx, or voice box.

lesion: A sore or other abnormality, generally on the skin.

metastasis: The spread of cancer from its initial location to other parts of the body.

Mohs surgery: A precise surgical technique used to treat skin cancer that involves progressively removing layers of cancerous tissue.

oropharyngeal cancer: Cancer of the back of the throat, including the base of the tongue and tonsils.

Pap smear: A preventive test that reveals the presence of an HPV infection on the cervix.

precancerous: Having the potential or likelihood to develop into cancer.

radiation therapy: Medical treatment that uses high-energy X-rays or other kinds of radiation to fight cancer.

screening test: A preventive medical test designed to look for signs of a disease or condition in a group of people who are at high risk of contracting the disease or condition.

speculum: A device that holds open the vagina during a medical exam or procedure.

trichloroacetic acid (TCA): An acidic solution applied by a doctor to treat genital warts.

vulva: The external female genitalia that surround the opening of the vagina. Includes the mons pubis, labia majora, labia minora, clitoris, bulb of vestibule, vestibule of the vagina, and Bartholin glands.

American Sexual Health Association (ASHA)
PO Box 13827
Research Triangle Park, NC 27709
(919) 361-8400
www.ashastd.org
ASHA describes itself as a trusted, nonprofit organization that advocates on behalf of patients to help improve public health outcomes. The organization delivers accurate, medically reliable information about STDs. Public and college health clinics across the United States order ASHA's educational pamphlets and books to give to clients and students. Community-based organizations depend on ASHA, too, to help communicate about risk, transmission, prevention, testing, and treatment.

Centers for Disease Control and Prevention (CDC)
1600 Clifton Road
Atlanta, GA 30333
(800) 232-4636
www.cdc.gov
The mission of the CDC is to protect people's health and safety, provide reliable health information, and improve health through strong partnerships. The organization offers a wealth of information about sexually transmitted diseases, including HPV, in pamphlets available by mail and on its website.

National Cancer Institute (NCI)

Public Inquiries Office
6116 Executive Boulevard, Room 3036A
Bethesda, MD 20892-8322
(800) 422-6237
www.cancer.gov
The National Cancer Institute supports research, training, the spread of health information, and other programs with respect to the cause, diagnosis, prevention, and treatment of cancer; rehabilitation from cancer; and the continuing care of cancer patients and the families of cancer patients. Its website contains extensive information about HPV as well as a live chat option that operates weekdays between 9 a.m. and 9 p.m.

National Library of Medicine MedlinePlus

8600 Rockville Pike
Bethesda, MD 20894
www.medlineplus.gov
MedlinePlus brings together authoritative information from the National Institutes of Health (NIH) and other government agencies and health-related organizations. MedlinePlus also has quizzes, videos, games, extensive information about medications, and the latest health news.

Planned Parenthood Federation of America

(800) 230-7526
www.plannedparenthood.org
Planned Parenthood is a nonprofit organization that provides low-cost or free reproductive health care services, sex education, and information to millions of people around the world. On the website, users can find a chat service so they can get answers to their sexual health questions as well as the address of the Planned Parenthood clinic closest to them.

FOR MORE INFORMATION

Books

Ambrose, Marylou, and Veronica Deisler. *Sexually Transmitted Diseases: Examining STDs*. Berkeley Heights, NJ: Jasmine Health, 2016.
Aimed at high school–age youth, this book offers information about sexually transmitted diseases, including the history of each illness, diagnosis, treatment options, and medical advances.

Corinna, Heather. *S.E.X: The All-You-Need-to-Know Sexuality Guide to Get You Through Your Teens and Twenties*, 2nd ed. Boston, MA: Da Capo Books, 2016.
S.E.X. clearly spells out what young adults need and want to know—with no shame, no judgment, and comprehensive and accurate information in clear, straightforward language.

Rushing, Lynda, et al. *Abnormal Pap Smears: What Every Woman Needs to Know*. Amherst, NY: Prometheus, 2001.
This book gives a straightforward presentation of the facts about Pap smears and how they can help diagnose HPV and other medical problems.

Staley, Erin. *HPV and Genital Warts*. New York, NY: Rosen Publishing, 2016.
Aimed at high school–age youth, this book offers helpful information for dealing with HPV and genital warts as well as strategies for prevention of future infections.

Websites

Cervical Cancer

www.cancer.gov/cancertopics/types/cervical
The main National Cancer Institute webpage about cervical cancer contains numerous useful links to websites providing a wide range of information about the disease.

Genital HPV Infection—CDC Fact Sheet

www.cdc.gov/std/HPV/STDFact-HPV.htm
This website gives an excellent general overview of the basic facts about HPV, including what it is, how it spreads, and how it can be treated.

InSpot

www.inspot.org
This website allows users to anonymously notify their sex partners that they have been exposed to a sexually transmitted disease. It also offers information regarding STDs and where to get tested.

Scarleteen

www.scarleteen.com
Geared toward teens and young adults, Scarleteen provides inclusive, comprehensive, and supportive information online about sexuality and relationships. The website offers a live chat or text option for one-on-one guidance and advice.

INDEX

A

abstinence, 42
American Cancer Society, 48, 67, 68–69, 74, 79
American Sexual Health Association, 12–13, 43
anal cancer, 22, 45, 65, 76–78
atypical squamous cells of undetermined significance (ASCUS), 31

B

basal cells, 16
Bethesda Classification System, 30
biopsy, 31–32, 57, 67, 70, 76, 78

C

cancer, defined, 65–67
cancers, HPV-related, 65–79
Centers for Disease Control and Prevention (CDC), 13–14, 17, 27, 28, 34, 35, 46, 50, 51, 54
cervical cancer, 6, 8, 45, 67, 68–74
    screenings for, 22, 26, 34–35, 68
    staging, 69–70
    statistics on, 22, 26, 65, 68
    strains of HPV and, 22, 68, 77
    treatment for, 70–72
Cervista HPV High-Risk DNA test, 34
chemotherapy, 67, 71, 72, 73–74, 75, 76, 77, 78, 79
colposcopy, 31–32, 57
condoms, and HPV prevention, 11, 35, 42, 63
cone biopsy/cold knife conization, 39–40, 42, 71–72
cryotherapy
    for lesions, 41–42
    for pre-cancer, 71
    for warts, 55, 61

N

National Institutes of Health, 26

O

oral cancers, 22, 35–37, 65, 77, 79

P

Papanicolaou, George N., 25, 26
Pap smear, 25, 26–27, 34, 38, 48, 49, 65, 67, 72
  anal, 27, 35
  explained, 28
  how often women should get, 27–28
  interpreting and understanding results, 28–31
partner, notifying about diagnosis, 82, 84
penis, cancer of the, 22, 65, 75–76
Perry, Rick, 52–53
Planned Parenthood, 31, 38, 41, 48, 55, 63–64
podofilox, 58–60
podophyllin, 58–60
precancerous cells, 24, 27, 30, 69, 71

R

radiation therapy, 67, 71, 72–73, 75, 77, 79
recurrent respiratory papillomatosis (RRP), 17

S

safe sex
  practicing, 35, 39, 42, 43, 63
  talking to partner about, 83–86
Sinecatechins, 60–61
Soranus, 7–8
STD screenings/testing, 19–20, 33
stigma surrounding STDs, 80–81
surgery
  for cancer, 67, 71, 75–76, 78, 79
  to remove lesions, 30, 31, 38–40, 42, 75

Michelle Harris was born and raised in Los Angeles, California. She studied at the University of California at Santa Barbara, where she received a bachelor of arts degree in psychology in 2008. She has worked as a digital content producer for several years, writing informational and marketing copy for television, online news, and consumer goods. She recently left the warm shores of Southern California for the bitter winters of Western New York, where she currently resides with her beloved dog, Zoey.